John J. Conklin's Account Book 1791

John J. Conklin's Account Book 1791

Edited and transcribed by
John R. Conklin, 2013

Epigraph Books
Rhinebeck, New York

John J. Conklin's Account Book 1791 © 2015 edited and translated by John R. Conklin

All rights reserved. No part of this book may be used or reproduced in any matter without written permission from the author except in critical articles and reviews. Contact the publisher for information.

Printed in the United States of America

Book and cover design by Colin Rolfe

Library of Congress Control Number: 2015960037

ISBN: 978-1-944037-15-4

Epigraph Books
22 East Market Street, Suite 304
Rhinebeck, NY 12572
(845) 876-4861
www.epigraphps.com

Summary

This journal contains 62 years of financial transactions from a 220 acre family farm in Hyde Park, Dutchess County, NY. The first entry is in 1791, the last in 1853. The account book was loosely divided by activities, (not chronologically by date), and shows entries for a sewing or tailoring business, farm product sales, the details of a two year building project (materials and labor), payments to schoolmasters for a son's education, and employment of both farm workers and domestic help. The account book contains hundreds of entries of customers, many of the names are relatives of "Uncle Johnny" Conklin who established the farm in 1751. He and his wife Maria were the parents of 13 children, 9 daughters and 4 sons. His first son, John J Conklin starts the book in 1791 and when he dies in 1803 the journal is taken over by his younger brother, Abraham I Conklin, who keeps it until his death in 1853.

    The book measures 8 1/2 inches by 13 inches and has three lined columns for recording the English Pounds, Shillings and Pence. It contains approximately 42 pages, however 10 pages have been removed by cutting. The entries are in ink, some very faded and almost illegible. The largest section contains the activity of the tailoring business (18 pages covering 11 years of data), with hundred's of names of customers. The hand writing is typical of the 1790's with confused "s" and abbreviations common for the period. The Account book records the use of Pounds/Shilling/Pence up until the 1830's, even though the Dollar currency was in effect. For example, one entry records borrowing $110 dollars and records it as 44 Pounds!

Provenance

The Conklin Family "homestead" was founded by Uncle Johnnie Conklin in 1751. He purchased 220 acres as part of Water Lot #1 in what is now the town of Hyde Park, NY. The boundaries of the farm form the town line of Pleasant Valley to the east and the town of Poughkeepsie to the south. The house is a center hall, two story, colonial with two large rooms with brick fireplaces on each end of the structure, with bedrooms above. An article published in the August 7 1886 edition of the "Pouhkkeepsie News-Telegraph" by a neighbor, Edgar Thorn, refers to him as "Uncle Johnnie" and describes his numerous "progeny". Uncle Johnnie's father arrived in Poughkeepsie in 1725, moving from Sleepy Hollow, and purchasing 770 acres in the vicinity of today's Poughkeepsie Rural Cemetery.

This book was found by my Grandfather, John B. Conklin, when he removed the "lean-to" structure attached to the main house about 1920. My father, Leland T. Conklin, passed the relic on to me. I had it digitally copied and then transcribed. We know the last entry was made June 6, 1853, but when it was stored in the "lean-to" structure is conjecture. It is possible that the "building" project recorded in this account book was the construction of the "lean-to" along with the summer kitchen with its fireplace and dutch oven. With all the people living in this

The "lean-too addition" is visible in background.

house in the 1790's, it would seem probable that the extra rooms provided by the "lean-to" were very much needed.

The Tailoring Activity

In 1791 when John J Conklin, age 29, takes over the management of the farm from his 66 year old father. There are 6 women at the homestead, 4 unmarried daughters of "Uncle Johnny", his wife Maria, and possibly, John J's wife Susan. The daughters are Sarah, age 27, Catharine, age 24, Hester, age 22 and Mary, age 18. It is assumed that some of these females handled the sewing activity. However, the 1790 Census shows only three females present in 1790. The identity of the household is unknown.

Each customer was accorded a line item with the product e.g. "sute of clothes", vest, overhals, etc. with the amount due. When the money was collected the entry was "X ed" out. Names were spelled phonetically, and sometimes the same person had several spellings. All the activity involved men's clothing, no woman's clothing ordered! All the activity was recorded in Pounds Sterling.

There are 18 pages of entries with and average of 22 entries per page. Typical activity lists "to making" vests, breeches, overhals, great coat, trowsers, and stick twists. (I am not sure of the definition of a "stick twist", but know it was associated with buttons). They charged extra for "buckram" and "hooks and eyes". Prices varied from customer to customer (because of size?) but examples are 6 to 7 shillings for a pair of overhals, 4 to 6 shillings for a vest, 8 to 10 shillings for a coat, 8 shillings for breeches. The exchange rate appears to be $2.50 to the pound. (12 pence equals one shilling, 20 shillings equals one pound, 1 shilling equals $.125)

Many of the customers were family related. The Storm, Travis, Patterson families were married to the Conklins. Female cousins married the Stoutenburghs and the Ackermans. The

Conklin male relatives were numerous. Between Uncle Johnny's 6 brothers and their offspring there were 36 male Conklin's, uncles or cousins to John J Conklin, the keeper of the accounts. There were 7 different Storm names. John J's wife was Susan Storm and his grandmother was Annatje Storm. I'm not sure if they were all related, but there is a good chance that many were.

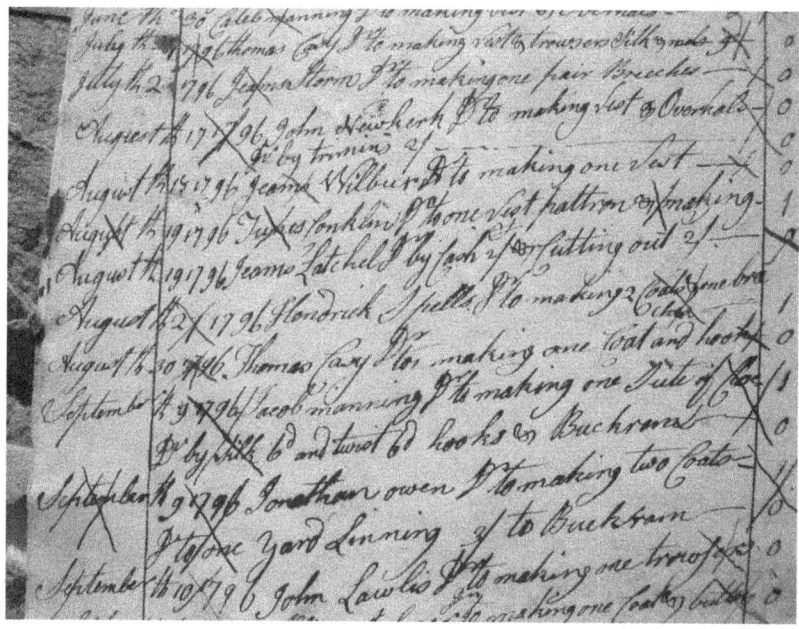

David Conklin, a brother to "Uncle Johnnie" and Uncle to John J was the most frequent customer. He was married three times, must have been a fancy dresser with the many vests and coats he ordered! He was their best customer!

In addition to the family related customers, (the many Conklins, Storms, Travis, Pattersons) there were a significant number of neighbors who purchased clothes.

Other names, at random, include Hall, Lewis, Schriver, Silvernails, Cook, Odell, Stoutenburg, Lattin, Echer, Angevine, Tomkins, Golder, Mott, Manning, Wilber, Thorn, Ward, Wigg, Sowl, Balding, Flagler, Wood, Moss, Hutchins, Green, Dorlon, Culver, King, Rider, Bennet, Thurston, Nelson, Cronk, Latchel, Casy, Owen, Palmer, Dusberry, Newkerk, Apells, Beneway, Pells,

Platt, Barlow, Williams, Amberman, Witman, Night, Foreman, Mead, Reccord, Irish, Weeks, Baker, Kilsey, Loder, Lowder, Acker, Taylor, Gooden, Vananden, Badgley, Lake, Reelding, Hunt, Barlow, Vandewater, Barnes, Cary, Hallick, Wright, Vall, Church, Happy, Carmon, Shear, Tuttles, Milkins, Husted, Eckert, Tarpanny, Bostick, Donlon, Tod, Flow, Valentine, Nash, Waff, Mors, Justice, Gorder, Petel, Smith, Porlin, Right, Meeks, Moss, Nelson, Owen, Spenser, VanWagner, Cain, Wiles, Venandon, Witman, Sagues, Disbrow, Lattony, Chan, Thuylon, Delren.

This business stopped after 11 years, in 1802. John J died in 1803.

The Building Project

John J Conklin kept a separate section in the Account Book to track the labor and materials that went into a two year building project. The first entry is August 29 1797 and the work that year continues until December 16 1797. There was no activity during the winter months. The work starts again on April 21, 1798 and is finished by July.

Joseph Mead of Pleasant Valley appears to be the lead carpenter with seven other workers listed. The daily rate is between 5 and 8 shillings. Three masons are listed at 8 shillings per day.

Pitch pine plank and shingles are 12 pounds, 12 shillings, and 6 pence. Seven pounds of nails cost 12 shillings. Bricks were purchased for 5 pounds, 10 shillings. Glass, nails, paint, hinges, thum latches, (his spelling), sash, lath are also listed and priced.

It is pure conjecture as to the nature of the project. My best guess is the summer kitchen addition on the east end of the main house. It had two doors front and back, two windows, a fireplace with a "dutch oven". This will account for the bricks, glass, lath etc. This was a rather small addition and should not take two years to complete. It is possible the "lean-to" addition may have been built at this time. This would account for the pine planks, shingles, and quarter boards. It would also provide needed sleeping space for the extended household.

Summer kitchen on right with fireplace and dutch oven

Farm Workers

John J Conklin begins to hire farm help in 1794. He hires Francis Leroy for one month. Next year, in August 1795, he hires Leroy for 2 months work at 3 pounds.

In 1796, he employs two workers, Robert Welsh and Abraham Kip. Kip works for 7 months at the rate of 1 pound, 2 shillings per month. Kip leaves in February 1797 but returns in December of 1798 at an increase in pay to 40 shillings per month. Of note, John J docks Kip for a half days work on October 15 1796 because he went to a horse race! (Where was this event? County Fair?)

In 1801, he pays Nathan Wigg for weaving cloth. The going rate was one shilling per yard. He bought 74 and 1/3 yards at that price.

Farm Product Sales

The first recorded sale is wool and buckwheat in 1793. Buckwheat is not a form of wheat, but the seed of a flowering plant. Buckwheat was a common product on colonial farms but its use steadily declined in favor of corn and rye grains.

In March of that year he sold 7 gallons of cider (sider) at one shilling per gallon. This means the apple orchard was planted around 1790? The apple orchard was still producing in the 1940s when I was a boy on the farm. The apples were Baldwin and Greenings, a hard long lasting storage apple.

In 1794 he records sales of hay, wheat, rye, and flax. Sales in 1795 include rye, buckwheat and a pig. In 1796 rye flour is 4 shillings per pound and bran is going for 2 shillings. In 1798, pork is 9 pence a pound and beef is 4 pence per pound. By 1801 corn has dropped to 6 shillings per bushel from 8 shillings in 1795.

There is very little recorded in the year 1802 and John J dies February 3 1803. His wife, Susan, must continue to live in the farm homestead with son William born 1800. The Account book shows compensation to John J's brother Abraham I for the education of William. It is not known if Susan remarried or when she and William left the place.

Abraham I. Conklin Takes Over

When John J's younger brother Abraham takes over the running of the family farm, he is 27 years old, and unmarried. His father, Uncle Johnnie, is 78, but still going strong (he lives to be 98). Abraham married Dorcus Briggs in December 5 1805 and will produce 4 children before he dies on 15 May 1853, age 77 years, 1 month and 22 days.

The account book is dormant for 26 years from 1802 until Abraham's first entry on March 8 1828. Abraham uses the book to record farm sales, workers he hires, and some financial transactions, which consist of Notes from relatives and others. In 1828 Abraham is 52 years old, and his son, John B. who remains on the farm, is 21 years old. Uncle Johnnie is still living at age 92.

Farm Workers

In March 1828, Anthony DuBois begins to work for Abraham for $9 per month plus keeping his horse. In 1832 William Wood works for 4 months and Elazson Cooper starts. Other names are Nathan Odell, Lewis DuBois, Jonah Freightenburgh, Oliver Nickerson, Andrew McMannis and Samuel Wood. Payments are in Dollars, the English pounds/shillings are starting to disappear, but in 1828 an entry still shows a $5.00 transaction recorded as 2 pounds. Old habits die hard!

Household Workers

In 1847 Eliza Clark and Eliza England start work. No compensation rate is shown. In 1849 Susan Wig is working. The last appears to be Maryann Beskins who started in 1851 and is still working when Abraham dies in 1853. The final entry in the Account book is June 6 1853 when Maryann is "paid in full".

Abraham's Farm Sales

The apple orchard was very productive by 1828. Many sales of cider (sider) by the barrel as well as "spirits" and one sale of a quart of "brandy". Cider was a shilling per gallon while brandy was a shilling per quart. (Note, still using Pound Sterling notations). Other sales listed bushels of corn, rye, wheat, oats. Seed buckwheat, and hay. In 1832 a "stack of hay" was $5.00, buckwheat was 50 cents and a load of wood sold for $3.00 It appears the conversion to Dollars finally took in 1832.

The harvest of wood was active for several years starting in 1832. A total of 60 loads for a total of $183.30.

Farm prices were lower in the 1830's than in the 1800's. Corn was 4 shillings per bushel versus 8 shillings in 1797.

Conclusions

The Account Book offers a valuable perspective of the farm economy in the late 18th Century and early 19th in Dutchess County.

The amount of tailoring business is a surprise for a farm economy. It means the women of the household were very active and productive. That activity produced far larger income than the farm product sales.

The "building project" offers a unique look at labor rates and cost of materials in 1797 and 1798.

The cost of William's education is recorded, but the amount of time is not noted and we lose the value of the Schoolmaster's day.

Farm labor rates offer a look at a laborers income in the 1800s. It is assumed that "food and board" were part of the compensation. However, workers were "docked" for sickness and days off.

Notes
Definitions of terms found in the Account Book

BUCKRAM: A coarse cotton or linen fabric heavily sized with glue, used for interlining in garments and stiffening in millinery. Also used in book binding.

BUCKWHEAT: A plant cultivated for its grain like seeds. It is not related to wheat, is not a cereal grass, but is related to sorrel, knotweed, and rhubarb. Originally "beech wheat" named after the triangular seeds which resemble the larger seeds of the beech tree. It is used like wheat. Buckwheat plants grow quickly, producing seeds in 6 weeks and ripening in 10 to 11 weeks. It was a common crop in the North East in the 1700's.

SILK TWIST: A twisted thread of 2 or more strands of silk. Used for making button holes.

BRAN: Bran is present in and may be milled from any cereal grain including corn, wheat, oats, barley, and millet.

SHOAT: A young pig just after weaning.

BROWN HOLLON: Unbleached Holland linen.

John J Conklin His Book
1791 September the 16 This book was made

November the 15 1791 then received of John Travis Jur for Sias
    Latting in cash   1-1-0

January th 3 1793 by cash   March March   0-8-0

July th 17 1792   Peter Storm credit by cash   2-0-0

October th 23 1792 by cash rec'd of Francis   0-10-0

October 19 1792   James Storm by cash   0-1-0

January th 11 1794 Cr by cash   0-8-0

May th 19 1796 by cash   3-6-6

April th 11 1797 Cr by cash   1-8-5

November th 8 1798 Cr by three bushels corn at 3/6   0-10-6

July th 5 1799 Cr by two bushels corn at 4/6   0-9-0

April th 19 1800 Cr by one ????? bushel   1-5-0

February th 24 1802   Jeams Storms Cr by Cash Ten Dollars 4-0-0

    13-18-5

    0- 6-0

                                                            6

                                                        14-10-5

November th 12 1798 Peter Schuryver Cr to 3 bushels
        Buckwheat   0-9-0
                Schryuver Cr to one bushel buchwheat   0-3-0

July th 5 1799 John Conklin Cr to bushel and half of wheat

January th 3 1793 Benjamin Latten Credit by cash   1-12-0

        John J Conklin
Seven Dollars ---- 2-16   Eight Dollars   3-4-0
                                     Ten Crowns   4-10-1
                                  20 Quarter dollars   2-0-0
                                          20 Dito   2-0-0
                            1. 9 Dito in order three ?? 0-
                                                        18-0
                                    2 Fifterreany ??   0-3-0

                                                        12-15-2

32 Bushels wheat at 8/
12-16 John J Conklin Db his name the same day Jeams Storm
        his name
        John ???? to pay or Calbse ??

5-2 Paid to Latchel for my father   0-6-0

                                                        13-1-2
                                                        12

Labor for ???? John J Conklin his name and hand
        to pay ????? to paid to John J Conklin   13-13-2

        John J Conklin his hand and ????

                        14

For value received   Db   ????

October th 19 1792 Isaac Travis Credit by cash lent John
    Conklin   0-15-0   John Conklin his hand
    hand ap???   Clinton the 24 ????
    Jacob Vanearey October the 24 1795

(new page)

November th 11 1791 Peter Storms Db to making coat and vest
    0-15-0

November th 19 1791 Nathan Wig Db to making one coat
    0-8-0

November th 23 1791 Jacob Bartley Db to making one coat
    0-10-0

November th 28 1791 ???? Scheryver Db to 2 coats and one
    breeches   0-17-0

December th 5 1791   James Vall Db to making one suit of
    clothes and coat and vest   1-4-0

December th 7 1791   John Wig Jur Db to making one vest
    0-4-6

December th 17 1791 David Conklin Db to making two coats
    0-14-0

December th 17 1791 Samuel Lewis Db to making one vest &
    thread   0-6-3

December th 24 1791 Mikel Tompkins Db to making three
    scanys thread and silk   0-6-6

January th 4 1792　　Charles Manning Db to making one suit of clothes and vest and overhals　　1-6-0

January the 6 1792　　John Odell Db to making great coat and two ?aylor coats and one pair breeches　　1-17-0

January the 9 1792　　William Balding Db to making one sute of clothes and great coat and vest　　1-3-0

January the 10 1792　　John Hall Db to making great coat
0-7-6

January the 11 1792　　Abraham D Conklin Db to making overhals　　0-4-0

January the 12 1792　　John Church Db to making Overhal & trowsers　　0-6-0

January the 13 1792　　Samuel Lewis Db to making one vest
0-5-0

Feburary the 6 1792　　Bot Hoocon Db to making one sute of clothes　　0-15-6

February the 17 1792　David Conklin Db to making 3 vests & one breeches　　0-18-0

March the 29 1792　　Albartis Schriver Db to two vests
0-18-0

March the 30 1792　　Jonathon Angvine Db to making vest & breches　　0-7-0

April the 7 1792　　Isaac Conklin Db to making two coats
0-11-0

April the 4 1792 John D Conklin Db to making one breeches & silk   0-5-8

April the 4 1792   Peter Schriver Db to making one breeches   0-6-0

April the 27 1792   William Stoutenbough Db to making two coats and one vest   1-4-0
William Stoutenbouh carried over from the old account two shillings   0-2-0

(new page)

May the 4 1792   Winot Silvernails Db to making two vests and one pair breeches & cutting   0-17-0

May the 9 1792   David Conklin Db to making vest & overhals   0-8-0

May the 14 1792   Isaac Conklin Db to making one vest   0-4-0

May the 16 1792   John Churchel Db to making coat & vest   0-16-0

May the 26 1792   William Cook Db to making vest and breeches and fitting one coat and trimmings   0-14-6

May the 29 1792   George Happy Db to making one suit of close   1-4-0

June the 4 1792   Fransis Storm Db to turning one coat   0-14-0

June the 8 172   John Carmon Db to making one coat   0-12-0

| June the 8 1792 | Prime Pellse Db to making vest & breeches | 0-12-0 |

| June the 13 1792 | James W Stoutenburg Db to making 2 coats | 1-0-0 |

June the 29 1792 Samuel Lewis Db to nankeen for ??? pair breeches   0-7-0
                                     to trimmings   0-3-10
Samuel Lewis to making one pair breeches   0-6-0

July the 2 1792 Lewis Shear schoolmaster Db to turning coat and vest   0-16-0

July the 4 1792 James Tuttles Db to making 1 sute of clothes   1-4-0

July the 7 n1792 Joseph Mott Db to making one pair overhals & & ??   0-6-6

July the 10 1792 Robert Milkins Db to making vest & breeches   0-12-0

July the 12 1792 Richard Conklin Db to turning one coat   0-9-0

July the 14 1792 John Church Db to making one suit of clothes drawers and overhals   1-11-0

July the 20 1792 John Storm Db to making one suit of clothes & thread to be answerd by Peter Storms   1-4-0

August the 23 1792 Joseph Husted Db to making one sute of clothes & twist   1-4-6

August the 31 1792   Benjamin Lattin Db to making one sute
    of clothes and one coat   1-4-0

September the 19 1792   Hendrick Echer Db to making
    one suit of clothes   1-4-0
    Db two ?? ji??ns silk & buckrom & hode ?   0-2-8

September the 28 1792   David Conklin to making vest &
    overhals   0-9-0

(new page)

October the 13 1792   James Storms Db to making one sute of
    clothes   1-3-0

October the 29 1792   Lewis Shear Db to making coat &
    breeches   0-18-0
    Db to hooks and one scein silk   0-1-0

September the 1 1792 Hendrick Eckert Db to making vest ?ree
    ?cheo   0-12-0

December the 14 1792 Jonathon Angevine Db to making one
    sute of clothes and coat and breeches   1-8-0

December the 20 1792 David Conklin Db to making two vests
                                                                0-8-0

January the 5 1793   Samuel Lewis Db to making great coat &
    overhals   0-13-6

April 22nd 1753   John Hunt Poughkeepsie Dutches
    County

January the 16 1793   Nathan Wig Db to making one coat
                                                                0-8-0

January the 19 1793   William Schriver Db to making coat &
    cutting   0-12-6

January the 24 1793   John Odell Db to making coat &
    breeches   0-16-0

January the 28 1793   David Conklin Db to making great coat
    & vest   0-12-0

February the 9 1793   Mike Tomkins to making vest and
    breeches   0-12-0
    Db to trimins & cutting out   0-3-0

February the 14 1793 John Tarpanny Db to making three sutes
    of clothes & great coat   3-8-0
    Credit by cash at the same time   2-0-0

                                                                      1-8-0

February the 18 1793 John Golder Db to making three coats
                                                                      1-6-0

March the 2 1793   Peter Van wagner Db to making one sute
    of clothes & trimmins   1-6-9

March the 18 1793   David Conklin Db to making two coats
    & two pair overhals and one stick twist   1-10-6

March the 21 1793   John Bostick Db to making one coat
                                                                    0-10-0
    for trimings   0-1-2

April the 17 1793   David Conklin Db to making coat and
    overhals & two stiks ??   0-15-0

April the 25 1793   Joseph Mott Db to making one overhals
                                                                    0-6-0

May the 25 1793   Peter Storm Db to making one breeches
                                                                          0-6-0

(new page)

June the 1 1793   Isaac Conklin Db to making three sute of
    clothes   2-17-0
    to one fasen & one buttons at 3/0   0-3-0

June the 5 1793   John Golder Db to making one pair
    breeches   0-6-0

June the 7 1793   Jeans Wilbur Db to making one coat
                                                                          0-9-0

June the 8 1793   Joseph Mott Db to making one vest 0-6-0

June the 11 1793   Charles Manning Db to making one sute
    of clothes great coat and vest   1-12-0

June the 22 1793   David Conklin Db to making one vest
                                                                         0-4-6

June the 27 1793   Charles Manning Db to making one coat
                                                                      0-11-0

Jult the 5 1793   Jonathan Angevine Db to making one
    sute of clothes   1-0-3

July the 27 1793   David Conklin Db to making coat and
    overhals and trimins   0-16-6

August the 22 1793   Benjamin Donlon Db to making coat &
    vest   0-11-0

August the 24 1793   John Ward Db to making one great ????
0-?-4

August the 30 1793   Stephen Thorn Db to making coat & vest
0-18-3

September the 17 1793 Peter Storm Db to making two coats
and one pair overhals   0-12-0

September the 24 1793 William Tod Db to making one coat
0-7-0

November the 5 1793 David Conklin Db to making vest and
two pair breeches & drawers   0-19-0

November the 9 1793 Simon Tarpanning Db to making vest
and breeches   0-12-0

November the 23 1793 John Golder Db to making one sute of
close and overhals & two vests   1-6-0

December the 4 1793 Francis Storm Db to making vest an twist
0-6-6

December the 7 1793 Samuel Lewis Db to making vest and
breeches   0-12-0

December the 7 1793 Jonathon Sowl Db to making one setut?
Coat   0-14-0

December the 10 1793 Lief Lattin Db to making one great coat
0-8-0

December the 18 1793 John Flow Db to making vest & breeches
0-13-0
Db to one scain silk a/8 to eight scains thread 0-1-4

(new page)

December the 21 1793 Nathan Wigg Db to making one pair of breeches   0-5-0

December the 31 1793 James Valentine Db to making two sutes of clothes & great coat and overhals   1-19-0
credit by cash at the same time   1-4-0

January the 18 1794   Samuel Lewis Db to making one coat and breeches   0-14-0

January the 24 1794   David Conklin Db to making one vest and two pair overhals   1-8-0

January the 25 1794   James Wilbur Db to making vest and overhals and twist   0-13-0

February the 13 1794 Isaac Conklin Db to making two sutes of clothes and coat and vest   2-10-0

February the 17 1794 David Conklin Db to making two coats and one vest   1-0-0

February the 22 1794 Philip Nash Db to making one sute of clothes and scain silk   1-6-6

February the 22 1794 Then Joshua Mors coat finisht   0-0-0

March the 7 1794   Laweance Waff Db to making three sutes of clothes one overhals one pair breeches   2-8-0

March the 14 1794   Jonathon Sowl Db to making one sute of clothes   0-16-0

March the 21 1794   Winant Silvernail Db to making three
    coats   1-10-0
    carried over his old account   0-2-0

April the 11 1794   David Conklin Db to making three vests
    great coat and overhals   1-7-0

April the 25 1794   Isaac Balding Db to making one coat
     0-6-0

May the 9 1794   Joshua Mors Db to making one sute of
    close   1-4-0
    to trimins   0-3-0

May the 13 1794   John Golder Db to making three sutes of
    close & one coat   2-13-0

May the 22 1794   Paul Flagler Db to making one coat
     0-12-0

May the 23 1794   Jeams Wilbur Db to making vest &
    overhals   0-12-0

(new page)

May the 31 1794   Elijah Mors Db to fasing one coat & mohasc
    Cr by cash at the same time   7 / 0-7-0

June the 2 1794   John Wood Db to making one vest
     0-4-6

June the 6 1794   Nathaniel Moro Db to making coat &
    vest   0-14-6

June the 12 1794   William Stoutenburgh Db to making 2
    vests & one pair breeches & 1/6 in cash   0-16-6

June the 26 b1794   Samuel Lewis Db to making I pair
    overhals   0-6-4

July the 1 1794   Peter Storm Db to making one pair
    breeches   0-6-0
    to silk and twist and thread 1/6   0-1-6

July the 3 1794   Theodorus Rider Db to making one pair
    overhals   0-6-0
    to twist and buttons   0-0-11

July the 8 1794   William Latten Db to making vest &
    breeches   0-10-0

July the 14 1794   Isaac Wood Db to making vest &
    breeches & twist   0-13-6

July the 21 1794   Peter Storm Db to two days raking &
    binding   1-8-0

July the 31 1794   Abraham D Conklin Db to making 1
    overhal & thread   0-6-6
    and one days raking & binding   0-8-0

August the 13 1794   Charles Justice Db to making one pair
    trousers and cutting out   0-5-0

August the 18 1794   John Gorder Db to making one coat &
    silk & buttons   0-10-6

August the 20 1794   Joshua Moss Db to making vest &
    breeches & twist   0-12-8

August the 3 1794   Jacob Hutchins Db to making vest and
    overhals   0-13-0

September the 1 1794 Abram Wood Jur Db to making one vest
                  0-4-6

September the 24 John Manning Db to making 2 vests &
 silk   0-9-6

October the 1 1794 Joseph Green Db to making one coat
                  0-12-0
 by cash at the same time 8/

October the 18 1794 Charles Manning Db to making one sute
 of closes   1-3-0
 and to making one vest and silk   0-6-0

November the 1 1794 David Conklin Db to making one
 overhals   0-6-0

November the 11 1794 Benjamin Dorlon Db to making three
 coats three vests & one pair overhals 1 stick twist & silk
                  0-18-10

November the 12 1794 Deter Petel Db to making one overhals
 & letting   0-7-0

November the 14 1794 John Petterson Db to making one coat
                  0-13-0
 to one dosen and nine buttons at 4/ 0-7-0

November the 18 1794 Samuel Smith Db to making breeches &
 thread and linning   0-6-6

(new page)

November the 19 1794 David Conklin Db to making one
 overhals   0-6-0
 to one scain silk & thread and large buttons 0-1-6

November the 2 1794 Jonathan Lowel Db to making coat vest & silk 0-18-6

November the 29 1794 Carried over from Winat Silvernails account 0-4-8

December the 6 1794 John Golder Db to making one coat two pair breeches vest and overhals 1-12-0

December the 26 1794 John Culver Db to sundries in clothes 1-13-0

December the 27 1794 Jeans Culver Db to making 4 coats & 2 pair breeches 1-8-0

December the 31 1794 Henry Lake Db to making 2 coats and vest 1-6-0

January the 8 1795 Isaac Balding Db to making two coats 0-16-0

January the 17 1795 Benjamin Porlin Db to making great coat & cutting 0-11-0

January the 31 1795 Peter Storm Db to making one coat and silk 0-16-0

February the 4 1795 Isaac Conklin Db to twelve & half days work 2-10-0

February the 10 n1795 Eljah Right Db to making overhals and silk & thread 0-8-0

February the 13 1795 John Silvernale Db to making one vest & ba??? 0-9-6

February the 20 1795   David King Db to making three coats
                                                                    1-5-0

March the 21 1795   John J Travis Db to making coat and vest
                                                                    1-0-0
    Db to two sticks twist and one scain silk and hooks
        &eyes   3

April 4 1795   Jeams Ackerman Db to making coat &
        breeches   0-19-0

May the 2 1795   Jacob Hutchins Db to making lappel coat
        & three and half   0-16-4
        yard buckram   0-1-6

May the 13 1795   Abraham D Conklin Db to making one
        pair breeches & trimins   0-9-0

May the 19 1795   Charles Manning Db to making 1
        overhals & silk   0-7-6

June the 30 1795   Samuel Smith Db to making 1 pair
        breeches & trimins   0-8-3

July the 1 1795   Elijah Right Db to making one overhals
                                                                    0-4-0

July the 2 1795   Jacob Manning Db to making one
        overhals   0-7-0

July the 10 1795   Peter Storm Db to making one coat &
        hooks & eyes   0-15-6

July the 14 1795   Nathaniel Wood Db to making one pair
        overhals   0-7-0

September the 5 1795 Elijah Right Db to making one sute of clothes   1-12-0

September the 9 1795 Benjamon Latting Db to making one coat and hooks   0-12-6

September the 14 1795 Jeanis Wilbur Db to making one sute of clothes & hooks and I stik twist   1-8-0

September the 19 1795 Ellick Meeks Db to making sailors coat & man???   0-5-0

October the 5 1795   Jeams Latchel Db to making one coat   0-16-0
Jeams Latchel to cutting out 5 coats & breeches 2 vests   0-15-0
By cash two shillings   0-2-0

(new page)

October the 31 1795   Nathaniel Moss Db to making vest and trimins   0-6-0

November the 5 1795 Efram Bennet Db to making vest & breeches & trimins   1-1-3

November the 18 1795 Theodorus Rider Db to making one pair breeches   0-8-0

November the 20 1795 Jacob Manning Db to making vest & overhals   0-14-0

December the 24   Henry Lake Db to two coats two vests one pair overhals & trim   2-12-4

January the 2 1796   Elijah Right Db to making watch coat &
    2 sceins thread   0-12-4

January the 5 1796   John M Thurston Db to making vest &
    breeches   0-15-0
    Db by trimins   0-2-4

January the 22 1796   Jeams Culver Db to making 5 coats vest
    & breeches buckram hooks and eyes   2-18-0

January the 22 1796   David Nelson Db to making watch coat
                                                            0-14-0

February the 6 1796   Charles Lewis Db to making one coat
                                                            0-16-0
        Db to buckram lining hooks & eyes and thread
                                                             0-3-6

February the 11 1796   Elijah Right Db to making one vest &
    silk   0-7-6

February the 12 1796   Jacob Hutchins Db to making vest &
    overhals & trimin   0-12-6

February the 16 1796   Nathan Wigg Db to making one coat 2
    scans silk buckram   0-16-3

February the 27 1796   Charles Manning Db to turning one coat
    7 trimins   0-16-3

March the 3 1796   Phillip Irish Db to turning one coat &
    trimins   0-17-9

March the 8 1796   William Stoutenburgh Db to making one
    sute of clothes   1-4-0

March the 29 1796   Isaac Travis Db by cash to George Philips
                                                                    0-11-5

March the 31 1796   Isaac Travis Db to making coat & vest
    one scain silk & hooks   1-4-9
    by cash at the same time ten shillings

April the 11 1796   Jesse Coon Db to making one sute
    ofclose & hook   1-4-6

April the 21 1796   Joseph Thurston Db to one vest   1-9-4
    and making one coat   0-16-0
    2 scains silk buckram hooks and eyes   0-2-4
    Large & small buttons   0-3-4

                                                              2-11-0

May the 26 1796   Jonathan Owen Db to cutting out   0-4-0

May the 27 1796   Jeames Cronk Db to turning one coat &
    buckram   0-16-9

June the 2 1796   Peter Storm Db to making one coat
                                                              0-13-0

June 3 1796   Ely Angevine Db making one sute of
    regimental   2-5-0
    Db to half dosen small buttons   0-0-0

June 11 1796   Matthew Spenser Db to making one sute
    of clothes & hooks   1-14-6

June the 14 1796   John Wood Db to making one sute of
    clothes & hooks   1-8-6

June the 18 1796	Nathaniel Wood Db to making 1 sute of clothes & hooks	1-8-6

June the 27 the William Baker begun to work

(new page)

	Jeams Latchel Cr by cash 8 shillings	
June the 28 1796	Jeams Latchel Db to making coat & breeches & hooks	1-4-6
	Db by trimins -- 3 /	0-3-0
June the 30	Caleb Manning Db to making vest & overhals	0-12-0
July the 1 1796	Thomas Casy Db to making vest & trowsers silk & hooks	0-12-9
July the 2 1796	Jeams Storm Db to making one pair breeches	0-8-0
August the 17	John Newkerk Db to making vest & overhals	0-12-0
	Db by trimins	2/ 0-2-0
August the 14 1796	Jeams Wilbur Db to making one vest	0-8-0
August the 19 1796	Tunis Conklin Db to one vest pattron & making	1-5-0
August the 19 1796	Jeams Latchel Db by cash 2/ & cutting out 2/	0-4-0
August the 27 1796	Hendrick Apells Db to making 2 coats & one breeches	1-8-0

August the 30 1796   Thomas Casy Db to making one coat and
    hooks   0-8-3

September the 9 1796 Jacob Manning Db to making one sute of
    clos   1-10-0
    Db by silk 6p and twist 6p hooks & buckram   0-3-0

September the 9 1796 Jonathon Owen Db to making two coats
                                                            1-8-0
    Db to one yard lining 3/ to buckram   0-5-0

September the 10 1796 John Lawlis Db to making one trowsers
                                                            0-4-0

September the ?? 1796 William Palmer Db to making one coat
    & buttons   0-17-0

September the 19 1796 Jeams Storm Db by cash ten dollars 4-0-0

September the 19 1796 Silvenus Wilbur Db by cash   4-0-0

September the 23 1796 Henry Dusberry Db to one vest   1-7-0

September the 28 1796 Hendrick Apells Db to making vest &
    breeches and trowsers one scain silk and four buttons
                                                            1-3-6

October the 22 1796   Joshua E Moss Db to making coat
                                                            0-16-0
    Db to buckram and hooks and eyes   0-1-9
    Cr by cash at the same time 8/

October the 29 1796   Jeams Cronk Db to making coat &
    breeches   1-4-0
    Db to one vest   1-9-0
    to three scains silk 1/6 to buckram and thread 1 /2
                                                            0-2-8

November the 2 1796 Jeams Latchel Db to cutting out   0-2-9

November the 12 1796 ??ouber Wilsy Db to making one overhal
    & silk   0-4-6

November the 12 1796 Isaac Travis Db to making vest & silk
    0-8-6

(new page)

November the 19 1796 Jacobus Beneway Db to making one vest
    0-7-0

November the 21 1796 Fransis Storm Db to turning one coat
    0-18-0
    September the 26 1800 Cr by cash /-12-0
    to trimins ---------------------------   0-3-9

November the 24 1796 Jonathon Owen Db to making 2 coats 2
    vests & one pair overhals   1-5-0

November the 30 1796 Jeams Lake Db to cutting out   0-8-0

December the 1 1796 Peter Van Wagner to making one pair
    overhals & silk & thread   0-9-4

December the 3 1796 Jeams Storm to making one pair breeches
    & ????   0-9-2

December the 5 1796 Ely Angevine Db to making vest &
    overhals   0-16-0

December the 17 1796 Nathaniel Wood Db to making vest &
    breeches   0-14-0

December the 23 1796 Jeams Storms Db to making one vest
0-8-3

December the 24 1796 John Cain Db to making vest & overhals
0-16-0

Db by trimins 0-4-0

January the 13 1797 Simon Pells Db to making one pair breeches
0-8-0

January the 13 1797 Hendrick Pells Db to making sundrey of clothes
4-12-0

January the 13 1797 Joseph Platt Db to making one great coat
0-12-0

Db to trimins 0-0-6

January the 24 1797 Joseph Green Db to making coat & vest
1-4-0

Cr by cash at the same time 17 (shillings) & 5 pence
0-17-5

February the 4 1797 Jeams Wiles Db to making one pair breeches
0-8-0

February the 6 1797 Jacob Manning Db to making one overhals
0-8-0

February the 7 1797 Peter Schriver Db to making one pair breeches
0-8-0

Db to two scains silk 0-1-0

February the 10 1797 Jeams Cronk Db to making one trowsers
0-4-6

Db to trimins 0-1-0

February the 10 1797   Abijah Barlow Db to making vest &
    overhals   0-16-0
    Db to trimins   0-1-6

March the 21 1797   John Cain Db to making one coat & to
    half yd buckram 1/3   0-16-0
    hooks & eyes and thread   0-2-0

March the 27 1797   Isaac Wood Db to making coat &
    breeches   1-1-0

April the 7 1797   Abijah Barlow Db to making one coat &
    thread   0-15-0

April the 28 1797   Thomas Casy Db to making one vest &
    trimins   0-9-2

May the 16 1797   Thomas Casy Db by work   2-16-0

May the 23 1797   Hendrick Pells Db to making vest &
    trowsers for prime & thread   0-13-3

(new page)

May the 26 1797   John J Storm Db to making Coat &
    trowsers   0-19-0
    Db to three scains silk half yd lining hooks & thread
                                                    0-4-3

June 1 1797   Peter Schriver Db to making one vest
                                                    0-8-0

June the 16 1797   Nathaniel Wood Db to making trowsers
    & silk   0-4-6

June the 24 1797   William Lattin Db to making overhals &
    silk   0-7-6

July the 4 1797　　　John J Storm Db by cash　　　0-5-0

July the 5 1797　　　Richbel Williams Db to making coat &
　　vest　　　　　　　　　　　　　　　　　　　　　　1-4-0
　　Db to trimins one yd lining 2/6 buckram 1/3 silk & twist
　　　　　　　　　　　　　　　　　　　　　　　　　　0-5-7

July the 7 1797　　　Nicholas Venandon Db to making
　　overhals　　　　　　　　　　　　　　　　　　　　0-8-0
　　Db to trimins 1 ???? 4/　　　　　　　　　　　　　0-4-0

July the 7 1797　　　Jeams Latchel Db to cutting out 3
　　garments　　　　　　　　　　　　　　　　　　　　0-3-0

July the 7 1797　　　Derick Amberman Db to cutting our
　　suet　　　　　　　　　　　　　　　　　　　　　　0-4-0

July the 15 1797　　 John Culver Db to making vest &
　　overhals　　　　　　　　　　　　　　　　　　　　0-13-0
July the 27　　　　　Nathan Wigg Cr to ???ing thirteen yd
　　and three quarters & half quarter to and linning at ?
　　　　　　　　　　　　　　　　　　　　　　　　　　0-14-0

July the 7 1797　　　Db by cash eight shillings

September the 9 1797　Joseph Thorn Db to making one sute of
　　clothes and hooks and eyes　　　　　　　　　　　1-12-6

December the 8 1797　Jeams Latchel Db to cutting 3 coats　0-5-6

December the 23 1797 Jeams Night Db to making two great
　　coats　　　　　　　　　　　　　　　　　　　　　1-4-0
　　and two vesta six shillings each　　　　　　　　　0-12-0

December the 27 1797 Thomas Witman Db to making vest &
　　overhals and drawers　　　　　　　　　　　　　　0-18-0

December the 28 1797 John J Storm Db to making one vest & silk 0-7-6

January the 6 1798 David Ring Db to making two sutes of clothes great coat & long cloke and silk 2-10-10

January the 11 1798 Isaac Travis Db to making great coat and twist 0-12-6

January the 15 1798 Joseph Green Db to making over vest 0-8-0

February the 9 1798 Isaac Foreman Db to making one coat & trimins 0-18-0

February the 16 1798 Isaac Hutchins Db to making 2 coats & overhals 1-14-0
Hutchins Db to trimins 0-1-0

February the 21 1798 Joseph Mead Db to making one coat 0-14-0
Db to linning and silk 0-1-0

March the 12 1798 Nathaniel Latting Db to turning one coat 0-14-0
Db to ????? silk /6 & twist /6 and thread /6 0-1-6

(new page)

March the 2 1798 Isaac Conklin Db to making sundries of clothing 2-14-0

March the 3 1798 Samuel Sigue Db to making one coat & cloath 0-9-0

April the 11 1798 & mat???/	William Williams Db to making one coat	0-15-0
April the 18 1798	John Reccord Db to making great coat & trimins	0-17-6
June the 2 1798	Jeams Latchel Db to cutting vest & overhals	0-2-0
June the 2 1798	Jeams Latchel Cr to one swil pail	
June the 7 1798	John Segues Db to 20 lath 18 feet in length fetched by Peter Schriver at / 8 p	0-13-4
June the 15 1798	William Latting Db to making one coat	0-16-0
	Db to trimins	0-2-0
June the 16 1798	Thomas Casy Db to making coat and vest	1-3-0
	to altering one coat & hooks & thread	0-6-0
July the 3 1798	Thomas Casy Db to making two overhals & silk	0-9-6
July the 9 1798	Johny Sagues Db making one sute of clothes	1-10-0
	Db to thread 10 p and hooks & eyes 6 p and buckram 6 p	0-1-10
July the 12 1798	John Lawless Db by cash fetcht by his aon Joseph	5-0-0
July the 17 1798	John Conklin Db to three days raking & binding	
July the 21 1798	Abraham Wood Db to raking & binding one day	

July the 28   Daniel Forman Db to making one coat
                                                        0-12-0

August the 3 1798   Abraham Wood Db to making one coat 1
    scain silk hooks & eyes   0-17-0

August the 4 1798   Joseph Thorn Db to making one sute of
    clothes   1-6-0

August the 23 1798   Joseph Thorn Db to making two vests &
                                                  0-14-0
    linning one of them   0-8-0

September the 29 1798 Philip Irish Db to making vest & altering
    coat   0-14-0
    to silk and twist and thread for the coat   0-1-4

November the 17 1798 Richble Williams Db to makinf one suit
    of clothes   1-8-0
    Db to 8 scains thread & buckram flannel hooks and silk
                                                  0-4-6

November the 23 1798 Tunis Conklin Db to making one coat
                                                  0-16-0
    to buckram buttons & silk   0-2-9

December 29 1798   Jeams Night Db to making 2 coats 2 pair
    of breeches   1-5-0
    to altering one coat & five scains thread 7 p 0-2-6

December the 29 1798 Jesse Weeks Db to making one coat
                                                  0-40-0
    Db to 8 scains thread & silk   0-1-2

January the 1 1799   Jeams Latchel Db to making one coat &
    breeches   0-17-6

January the 1 1799   John Wood Db to making one coat &
    one scain silk   0-16-6

(new page)

January the 12 1799   John Conklin Db to making one sute of
    clothes and vest and three sticks twist   1-11-0

January the 17 1799   William Latchel Db to making one coat
    0-16-0
    Db to buckram & silk and Thread and buttons
    0-1-3

January the 19 1799   Samuel Baker Db to making one vest &
    linning   0-7-6

January the 23 1799   William Barns Db to making one suit of
    clothes & overhals & silk and eight scains thread
    1-11-2

January the 26 1799   Joseph Weeks Db to making one pair
    coverhals   0-7-0
    Db to 14 buttons ½ and 6 scains thread 6 p   0-1-8

February the 2 1799   Nathaniel Lattony Db to making two
    coats one trowsers   1-16-0

February the 2 1799   Henry Disbrow Db to turning one coat
    0-14-0
    to one yard holland 3/3 3 scains twist ?/6 & thread 6 p
    0-5-0

February the 5 1799   Peter Storm Db to making one coat
    0-12-0

February the 8 1799   Jony Kilsey Db to making one great coat
                                                              0-10-0
    Db to one scain silk & 6 scains thread   0-1-0

February the 19 1799   Jony Kilsey Db to making one sute od
    clothes   1-8-0
    Db to eight scains thread and linning /4   0-1-0

March the 5 1799   John Patterson Db to making one vest
    silk & twist   0-7-0

March the 8 1799   James S Storms Db to making one vest,
    silk & linning   0-8-0

March the 12 1799   John Conklin Db to making one sute of
    clothes & ???   1-2-6

April the 1 1799   Joseph Green Db to making coat &
    breeches & one scain & silk   1-2-0

April the 3 1799   William Loder Db to making one sute of
    clothes   1-4-0
    to making one sailor vest   0-7-0
    Db to to eighteen scains thread & twist one silk   0-2-6

May the 3 1799   Abraham A Wood Db to making one
    vest   0-6-0
May the 4 1799   Jeams P Stormn Db to making one coat
                                                              0-14-0
    Db to half yard buckram   0-1-0

May the 10 1799   William Latcher Db to making one vest
    & thread   0-4-2

May the 11 1799   William Lowder Db to making vest &
    trowsers   0-10-0

	Db to eight scains thread and one stick twist	0-1-2

May the 13 1799	Hendrick Acker Cr to weving 47 yards to cloath	2-7-0

May the 18 1799	Hendrick Acker Db by cash	1-4-0

May the 18 1799	Jesse Weeks Db to Nankeen	0-11-6
	to making vest & breeches	0-12-0
	to yard & quarter hollan at 3/	0-3-9
	to buttons silk & twist & thread	0-5-4

(new page)

June the 1 1799	John Patterson Db to altering one coat	0-16-0
	Db to dosen buttons at 2/ one stick twist /6	0-2-6

June the 15 1799	John Sigue Db to cutting out	0-3-0

June the 25 1799	Isaac Travis Db to making one vest & twist	0-6-6

June the 28 1799	Jeams Storm Db to making one vest & twist	0-7-6

June the 29 1799	Dolph Latting Db to making one sute of cloths	1-5-0
	and altering one regimental coat and three sticks twist 1 silk	0-10-0

July the 1 1799	William Latchel Db to cutting out	0-1-6
	& Dolph Latton Db to quarter of yard carsimeerat 17 at four yards	0-4-3
	Credit by cash at the same time eight shillings	

July the 6 1799   Gilbert Lewis Db to making vest &
    trowsers   0-10-0
    to one yard linning 3/ one stick twist one scain silk
    thread and buttons   0-6-2
    by cash of Lewis eight shillings   0-8-0

July the 8 1799   Isaac Conklin Cr by seven pound wool at
    2/6

July the 13 1799   Abraham I Conklin Db to making one
    coat   0-12-0

July the 22 1799   John Conklin Db to six days raking and
    binding

July the 27 1799   John Wood Db to making one vest
                                                          0-6-0

August the 13 1799   John J Gooden Db to making coat & vest
    & linning   0-19-0

August the 31 1799   Reberd Taylor Db to making coat & 2
    vests   1-4-0
    Db to trowsers   0-5-10

September the 20 1799 Polerd Ausber Db to turning one coat
                                                          0-16-0
    Cr by cash 8/ to seating breeches   0-8-3
    Db to trimins   0-2-3

December the 2 1799 John Wood Db to making one vest & silk
                                                          0-7-6

December the 21 1799 Philip Irish Db to making one vest   0-7

December the 25 1799 Henry Lake Db to making one coat &
    vest   1-3-0
    Db to one scain silk and buckram & cloth   0-2-9

December the 25 1799 Abraham A Wood Db to making coat
                                                                              0-16-0
    and amking one pair overhals   0-5-0

January the 2 1800   Aron Vananden Db to making great coat
                                                                                0-10-0

January the 7 1800   Joseph Mead Db to making one coat
                                                                                0-16-0
    Db to one scain silk and four scains thread   0-0-10

January the 10 1800   Joshua Badgley Db to making vest &
    overhals   0-12-0
    Db to ¾ yards holland brown at 3/ I stick twist & thread
    & buttons   0-3-10

January the 11 1800   Abraham A Wood Db to making vest &
    silk   0-7-6

(new page)

January the 16 1800   John Lake Db to making one coat 0-10-0
    Db to cutting out one sute of clothes   0-4-0

January the 17 1800   John Sagues Db to making one overhal
                                                                                    0-5-0
    Legues Db to silk /6 buttons twist and linning 1 / 4
                                                                                     0-1-10

January the 18 1800   Samuel Reelding to making vest   0-7-0
    Db to two sticks twist   0-1-0

January the 21 1800   Jeams Latchel Db to cutting 2 coats 0-4-0

February the 6 1800   John Hunt Db to making one coat 0-13-0
    credit at bthe same time 8/ shillings

February the 20 1800   Joshua Badgley Db to making one coat
    and thread   0-18-0

February the 25 1800   Nathaniel Latting Db to making vest and
    overhals and thread   0-12-4

March the 21 1800   Isaac Conklin Db for work   2-10
    Db for silk and twist and pins   0-3-10

March the 22 1800   Abraham Patterson Cr to sixteen days
    and half work at thirty nine shillings per month   1-4-9

April the 11 1800   Joseph Thorn Db to making breeches &
    hos ?   0-9-6

April the 12 1800   Bige Barlow Db to making vest &
    overhals   0-11-0
    to half yard linning 1/6 one scains silk 6/ and thread 6/
    and buttons   0-3-0

May the 17 1800   William Lauder Db to seating overhals
                                                 0-2-0

May the 30 1800   Jeams Latchel Db to cutting coats   0-2-6

June the 7 1800   John Golder Db to making vest &
    overhals & twist & cutting   0-12-6

June the 21 1800   Peter Storm Db to making one coat
                                                 0-16-0

June the 5 1800   Benjamin Vandewater Db to making one
     coat and thread   0-10-6

June the ? 1800   John Travis Db to making one coat & silk
                                                  0-14-6

July the 10 1800   Isaac Conklin Db to making vest & 2
     pair breeches   0-17-0

July the 12 1800   William Chan Db to making one coat
     and thread   0-12-4

July the 31 1800   William Lauder Db to making one suit of
     clothes and one pair trowsers   1-13-0
     Db to half yard brown hollen 1/9 and thread 1/6   0-3-3

August the 23 1800   David King Db to making one sute of
     clothes   0-16-0
     Db to one yard j?r?chen at 3 / 4   0-3-4

August the 24 1800   Isaac Conklin Db to making one pair
     breeches   0-6-0
     to silk and twist   0-1-0

(new page)

August the 29 1800   Hendrick Acker Db to making one sute
     of clothes   1-4-0
     Db to three sticks twist & three scain silk 0-3-0

December the 5 1800 Isaac Travis Db to making ano pair
     breeches   0-8-0

December the 13 1800 Joseph Thorn Db to making great coat
                                                  0-14-0

December the 13 1800 Abraham Patterson Db to making great
  coat   0-14-0
 Abraham Patterson Cr by cash (pound) 4

December the 20 1800 John M Thuylon Db to making three
  coats   1-4-0

December the 27 1800 Thomas Cary Db to making vest &
  panteloons   0-13-0
  Db to three buttons and thread   0-1-0

December the 30 1800 John Hunt Db to making one coat &
  twist   0-12-6

January the 6 1801 John Hunt Db by cash 0-2-6

January the 7 1801 Hendrick Acker Db to making one sute
  of clothes   0-6-0
  to thread & buttons 1 / 4   1-7-4

January the 17 1801 Joseph Thorn Db to making one sute of
  clothes (pound) 1-12 hooks and buckram 1 / 3 1-13-3

January the 17 1801 John Wood Db to making one vest 0-7-0

January the 23 1801 Joshua Barns Db to making one
  conslosun ?   0-18-0
  Barns Db to cutting & silk   0-4-6

January the 29 1801 Philip Irish Db to making one coat & silk
                     0-6-6
  Db to cutting out   0-2-0

March the 12 1801 Daniel Delren to altering pair breeches
                     0-2-9

April the 4 1801 William Barnes Db to making Coat & silk 0-15-0

April the 13 1801 Joseph Storm Db to making one breeches 0-8-0

Db to drays 1/6 one quarter ratinet 1/ one scain silk /6 0-3-0

and pockets 0-1-0

June the 2 1801 Jonathan Sowl Db to great coat & breeches 0-18-0

to one and half yds hollin at 3/2 and one scain silk 0-4-9

June the 8 1801 William Lowder Db to making one trowsers 0-4-3

June the 9 1801 Thomas Cary Db to making 1 trowsers silk & thread 0-5-6

July the 4 1801 Abraham A Wood Db to making coat & pantilloon 0-18-0

to one yard hollin 3/ one stick twist 2 scains silk & thread & buttons and buckram 0-5-11

July 25 1801 Samuel Thurston Db to making one coat 0-16-0

Db to trimins one scain silk 2 buttons & buckram 0-1-4

July the 28 1801 David Barnes Db to making one vest 0-7-0

August the 17 1801 Charles Manning Db to making one coat 0-16-0

to buckram 1/3 silk & twist 1/6 buttons & hooks 1/ 0-3-9

(new page)

September the 8 1801   Abram Patterson Db to making one coat
                                                         0-16-0
    to one yd hollen 3/ buttons 1 / 2 silk & buckram 1/3
                                                         0-5-6

October the 3 1801   Jonathan Sowl Db to making one coat
                                                         0-16-0

October the 8 1801   Jeams Lathel Db to making one vest &
    silk & thread   0-7-6

October the 10 1801   Joseph Thorn Db to making coat &
    trowsers   0-9-0
    Db to one dosen buttons 1/ 3 sticks silk & twist   0-2-6

October the 16 1801   John Thorn Db to making vest &
    overhals   0-14-0
    Db to silk and twist   0-1-0

October the 24 1801   William Latchel Db to making coat &
    vest   1-3-0
    Db to one scain silk buckram cutting & thread   0-3-0

October the 28 1801   Jeams Latchel Db to cutting one coat
                                                         0-2-0

October the 31 1801   Jonathon Sowl Db to making one coat &
    silk   0-14-6

November the 13 1801 William Lowder Db to mending and
    thread   0-4-6

November the 11 1801 Isaac Travis Db to altering one coat 0-4-0

November the 13 1801 Esekel Beneway Db to twist thread
    buckram cutting   0-2-6

November the 13 1801 Thomas Cary Db to seating overhals
0-2-6

November the 21 1801 Jonathan Sowl Db to making great coat
0-12-0

November the 24 1891 Abraham Patterson Db to making vest
0-7-0
    Patterson Db to trimins   0-7-0

November the 30 1801 Elijah Hallick Db to making trowsers
    and trimins   0-4-9

December the 2 1801 Thomas Cary Db to making pantiloons
0-6-0
    Cary Db to linning 1/6 and other trimins 1/   0-2-6

December the 2 1801 Elijah Wright Db to altering one coat &
    silk and cutting   0-9-0

December the 5 1801 John Thorn Db to making great coat
0-14-0

January the 19 1802   Joseph Thorn Db to making 2 sutes of
    clothes   2-14-3

January the 28 1802   Samuel Baker Db to making one sute of
    clothes   1-9-0
    Baker Db by trimins   0-5-8

January the 28 1802   William Lowder Db to mending   0-0-9

February the 6 1802   Isaac Travis Cr by cash   2/6

February the 12 1802 Abraham A Wood Db to making coat &
    vest   1-4-0

Wood Db 3 scains silk and twist 1/6 & buttons &
buckram   0-2-10

February the 24 1802   Peter Storm Db to making coat and
     breeches and cutting   1-7-0

February th 24   Jeams Storm Db to making great coat
                                                           0-14-0

(new page)

February 17th 1802   James Latchel Db to making great coat
     and breeches and cutting & hout   1-3-6

June 12th 1802   Joshua Barnes Cr by cash   0-16-0

August 10th 1802   John Thorn to making coat and
     pantaloons Db to hemming   0-19-6

(note end of tailoring business)

(new page)

New Section

March 8 th 1828   Then Anthony Dubois began to work for Abraham I Conklin for one year at the rate of nine dollars for Mo and hacking one horse upon hay and grass   43-4-0

May 6th 1828   Nathan Odell Db to A I C

May 14th 1828   to one barrel of sider   0-14-0

June 1st 1828   to two bushels wheat at 1 / 1   0-16-0
    paid   Db to ½ bushel of corn 4 . 6   0-2-3
    Db to 2 anvil blocks   0-8-0

November 6th   to 2 bushels rye at 5 (shillings)   0-10-0
    Db to ½ bushel of corn   0-2-6

December 20 th 1828   to cash 35 cents   0-2-0
    Db to one bushel of wheat at (shilling) 11   0-11-0
    Db to one bushel of corn   0-5-0

January 6th 1828   to half gallon spirits   0-3-6
    Db ½ gallon   0-3-6
    Db ½ gallon   0-3-6
    Db ½ gallon sent by McCone   0-3-6
    Db to five lb of beef   0-2-0

February 12th 1829   then balance & accounts between Aber I Conklin & Nathan Odell remains due to said Odell   0-9-6

February 12th 1829   Received payment in full Nathan Odell
                                                          0-9-6

(new page)

Anthony Dubois Db to Abraham I Conklin
    June 6th 1828 to cash lent? $10   4-0-0
    Db to cash $ 5 for Daniel Platt   2-0-0

September 5th 1828   Cash $5 to the training to flats??   2-0-0

September   to cash to go to Long lines ??? $2.50
                                                          1-0-0
    Db to cash to the Reding Party   4-0-0

July 12th   to cash $3 to the valley for ????   1-4-0

August 18   to cash $5 Dollars   2-0-0

November 18   cash paid to W. V.dewatr for Anthony
    Dubois Db   3.11.7
    for interest and horse keeping   3-11-7
    Db to cash twelve shillings   0-12-0
    Db by cash five dollars Christmas   2-0-0

January 1st 1829   to two bushels of oats   0-6-0

January 12th   to one bushel of oats   0-3-0
    Db to half bushel of oats   0-1-6
    to cash ten dollars to pay dilony ??   4-0-0
    to cash paid for one hary ?? of mittins   0-5-0
    to ½ bushel of oats   0-1-6

January 21st   to half bushel of oats   0-1-6

February 1st   to half bushel of oats   0-1-6

February 3rd	to cash five dollars at the ???ing for horse
                                                                    2-0-0
   paid 20th to cash $10 for to pay for boots & shoes 4-0-0

(new page)

March 29th 1830	then balance accounts between Abrm I
    Conklin & Nathan Odell amt received payment in full
    of Abrm I Conklin   4-0-0

April 6th 1830	Nathan Odell to Abrm I Conklin

April 6th 1830	1/ lbs of pork at 6	0-3
   Db to one gallon of sider	0-1
   Db to four lbs pork & I gallon sider	0-2
   Db to one barrel of sider	0-16
   Db to cash four shillings for his father	0-4
   Db to one bushel of corn	0-4

May 4th	to one gallon sider	0-1
   Db to one gallon sider	0-1
   Db to one gallon sider	0-1
   Db to one bushel of corn	0-4
   Db to one gallon of sider	0-1
   Db to one gallon of sider	0-1

September 3rd	to one barrel of sider	0-8

September 18th 1830 then balanced accounts with Nathan
    Odell remains due to A I Conklin one shilling & 11
    (pounds)   11-1

November	to one jug of sider	0-1
   Db to one gallon sider	0-1

December 4 1830	to one gallon sider	0-1

Db		0-1
Db		0-1
Db		0-1
January 1831	to one gallon of sider	0-1
Db I gallon		0-1
Db 1 gallon		0-1

(new page)

January 8th 1831	to one gallon sider	0-1-0
Db 1		0-1-0
Db 1		0-1-0
Db 1 gallon sider		0-1-0
February 1st 1831	to one gallon of sider	0-1-0
February 1	to half of a beef Wt 271 lb at 3 per lb	
		3-5-0
Db one gallon sider		0-1-0
Db one gallon sider		0-1-0
March 29	to one gallon sider	0-1-0
April 16th I	one Qt sider brandy	0-1-0
Benjamin Fuld Cash shoe mending		0-5-6

August 13th 1831

August 13th	to cash fifty cents	0-4-0
August 29th	Db to cash to get to Rynebeck $1	0-8-0
September 3rd	Db to cash to go to Hyde Park $3	1-4-0
October 6th	By cash three shillings	0-3-0

Ely Angevine Db to A.I.C. One side of beef 144 lbs at 3 lbs

    4-32

(new page)

July 1st 1831	Daniel Lattin Db to Abraham I Conklin	
July 1st	Daniel Lattin Db to cash $23	9-4-0
July 6th	Db to cash $6	2-8-0
July 8th	Daniel Lattin Db by cash $10	4-0-0
August 13th	Daniel Lattin Db by cash $10	4-0-0
August 24th 1831	Daniel Lattin Db by cash $10	4-0-0
October 5th	By Cash 6 shillings	0-6-0
October 6th	By cash thirty dollars $30	12-0-0
November 2nd 1831	then setled with Daniel Lattin up to this date remains due to Lattin	0-4-3
November 8th 1831	Cash paid this Susan Lattin in full	3-0-0
December 4th 1831	Cash paid Samuel Cullin $7 in full	
March 10th 1846	Jonah Freigtenburgh begin to work for Abraham I Conklin	$-3-0
May 21st	Db to cash $3	$-3-0
June 12th	Db to cash $2	$-2-0
July 8th 1846	Db to cash to go to town	$-5-0

1846 Db to cash for one shall ??		$-5-0

July   Db to cash to the pedler   0-0-?

December 7th 1846   Oliver Nickerson begun to work for
        Abraham I Conklin at $5 per

October   lost time to four days wedding   0-4-0
    Db half day Poughkeepsie   ½
    Db half day Poughkeepsie   ½
    Db one day verispise ??   1
    Db half day Poughkeepsie   ½
    Db half day town with Ciagan ? Poughkeepsie   ½
    Db half day town with Eliazaam   ½
    half day Poughkeepsie   ½
    Half day to vendue   ½
    to one day when moving furniture   1-0

(new page)

January 1 st 1832   William Wood Cr by 4 months work at
    $11 dollars per month   17-12-0

March 18th 1832   Cash for work $24   9-12-0

                                                   27-4-0

March 18th 1832   then paid William ??ed $15   6-0-0

October 8th   Elazson Cooper begun to work for
        bostom I Conklin at 75 per ????
    Elazons lost ime 3 ½ days wedding   3 ½
    Db one day New Years   1
    Db to six ½ days to Poughkeepsie   6 ½
    Db ½ day Poughkeepsie   ½
    to one day Henry Wrights

Elazson	Db (shillings) 22 to cash from dollars	
		$-?-0
	Db to cash from Shillings	$-0-50
	Db to cash 12 ½ cents	- -12 ½
	Db to cash to Poughkeepsie	$ -4-0
February 11th	Db to cash $3 dollars	$-3-0
Oliver	Db to cash $18 February 6th	$-??-0

(new page)

June 8th 1847	Samuel Wilber Cr by work	$-6
	to one day shearing sheep	- - 75
July 23	Cr by three days work in hay	$-3
July 26th	by one day in oats	½ 4

(new page)

	Cr By two days planting corn Oliver Nick	$ 1-25
	Oliver Cr by 4 ½ days in hay	4-50
	2nd Week Cr by 2 ¾ Days in hay	4-50
	3rd Week Cr by half day 2.75	½ 0.50
	4th Week Cr by five days	5
	5th Week Cr by two days work	$ 2.00

		$20.50
Paid in Full		7.56

	Remains Due Nickerson $13.94 cash	13.94
Oliver Nickerson Cr by 5 days work at 50 c		$2.50
Oliver	Cr by 5 days corn	2.50

Oliver	Cr by 3 days work	1.75

		$ 6.75

December 7th   Joseph Wood begun to work for Abraham I Conklin

January 9th 1848	Joseph Wood Db to cash	8.8
	Joseph Woods Lost time	½
	half day after his Chest	½
	half day to Poughkeepsie	½
	half day Christmas	½
	to one day sick	1
	to one day to John Woods	1
	Db Xmas day to Poughkeepsie	1
	Db to three days to three wedding	3

(new page)

April 6th 1847	Oliver Nickeson Db to Abraham I Conklin	
April 6th	Db to one bushel of potatoes	$ .75
May 8th	Db to three bushels of potatoes & 3 of oats	$3.56
August 7th	Db to cash three dollars	3.00

Eliza England Db by five days to Hyde Park	5
Eliza England Db by one day lost to Wright	1
Eliza England Db to two ½ days lost Christmas	2 ½
Eliza England to lost time to see her mother & to Wrights	10

| Eliza England to her Grandfathers funeral 5 days | 5 |

(page ripped and part missing)

April 6th 1847	Eliza Clark begin to work for A.I.C.	
May 2nd 1847	Db to cash paid Eliza Clark	$ 3.00
June 24th	Eliza England begin to work for Abraham I Conklin	
July 13th 1847	Eliza England Db to cash $ 1	$1.00
October 1st 1847	Eliza England Db to cash $5	5.00
October	Db to cash two dollars	2.00
	Db to cash for Maryann	.48
November 20th	Db to cash three dollars	$3.00
	Eliza England Db to cash Christmas $6.00	6.00
	Eliza Db to cash to pay Maryann $1.00	1.00
	Eliza England Db to cash $3 when she went to Wrights	$3.00
May 17th 1848	Db to cash $16.77 cents in full to pay	$16.77

(new page)

Eliza England	Db by two days to Wrights	2
March 14th 1849	Db by two & half to Wrights days lost	2 ½
April 20 th	Db to two days lost to Henry Wrights	2
	Db to half day lost to Henry Wrights	½

Db one day to Henry Wright	1

Eliza England lost time 5 days lost to her Grand fathers funeral – lost Wrights	5

July 4th 1848	Db to four days & half to	4 ½
	Db to one and ½ day to Wrights	1 ½

September 3rd	Db to 1 ½ days lost to Wrights	1 ½
	Db to six days & half lost time to Wrights	6 ½

Eliza England	Db to lost time New Years 8 ½	8 ½
	Db to one day to Henry Wrights lost	1
	Db to two and half days to Henry Wrights	2 ½

July 12 1848	Eliza England Db to cash	$ 1.00

August 22nd 1848	Eliza England Db to cash	$ 6.00

October 20th 1848	Eliza England Db to cash	7

September 11th	Eliza England Db to cash	3.00
	Eliza England Db to cash New Years $ 5	5.00
	Eliza Db to cash April 9th 1849 five dollars	5.00
	Eliza Db to cash May 9th 1849 to Henry Wright	7.00
	Eliza Db to cash June 8th 1849 two dollars	2.00
		5.0
	Db to cash to Henry Wright $2.50	2.50

		2.0

July 8th 1849 then balance accounts with Eliza England remains due to Eliza England two dollars	$2.00

Eliza England Db to ½ day lost time	½
Eliza England Db to 6 days lost to Henry Wright	6

(new page)

Lewis DuBois lost time May 22 one day to Poughkeepsie	1
June 28th 1847 to four days lost time when home	4
July 5th Db to seven days lost sick and ant hony ??	7
August 14th Db to one day lost Poughkeepsie	1
August 16th 17. 18. 19th 4 days lost	4
Db to lost time to the fare	1
Db to ½ day to town election	½

April 1st Andrew Mc Manny begun to work for Abrm I Conklin for eight months at $ 12.50 per mo

Andrew McManny Db to cash five dollars	$ 5.00
Db to cash to Poughkeepsie	6
December 6th 1848 Andrew McManny Db to cash	20
April 1st 1849 Andrew McManny Db cash in paid ?? in full ??	

Andrew McManny begun to work for Abraham I Conklin
    December first 1849 for one year for $ 12.5   125.00

    A.I.C.

Andrew Mac Manny   Db to cash nine dollars October 26th to
    the General Training $ 9

	& Db to cash to Poughkeepsie fifteen dollars	15
April 22nd	to cash in full	$17
		100

Andrew McMannes begun to work for Abraham I Conklin December 1st 1849 for one year for $12.5   12.5

July 10th 1850	Andrew McManny Db to cash $8.00	8.00
November Db to cash 75		0.75
November 30th 1849	Db to cash $15	15
February 18th 1851	Andrew Db to cash 10	$ 10.00
June 30th 1851	Andrew McMannes Db to cash $1	$ 1.00
July 30th 1851	Andrew McMannes Db to cash $10	$10
September 23rd 1851	Andrew McMannes Db to cash 20	20
February 12th 1852	Andrew McMannes Db to cash	$60

(new page)

April 5th 1847 Lewis Dubois begun to work for Abraham I Conklin

April 28th	Db to cash paid to the shoemaker	
		$00.12 ½
May 6th	Db to cash paid for tobacco	00.12 ½
May 22nd	Db to cash ten dollars	$10.00

July 5th	Db to cash five dollars	5.00
August 14th 1847	Db to cash five dollars	5.00
October 7th 1847	Db to cash four dollars	$ 4.00
November 20th	Db to cash two dollars	$ 2.00

November 29th 1849 Abraham I Conklin due Andrew
    McManney $ seventy six dollars $ 76.00
    cash paid McManny seventy six dollars in full   76.00

July 8th 1850   Mary Murphy Db to Abraham I Conklin
    Db to cash 12 ½ cents $ .12 ½
    Db to cash $4   4.00
    Db to cash 25 cents   0.25
    Db to cash 25 cents   0.25
    Db to cash 18 ½ cents   0.18 ½
    Db to cash eight shillings   1.00

October 27th 1849 Susan Wig begin to work for A.I.C.

Susan Wigs Db to 6 ½ days lost time		6 ½
Oliver Nickerson	Db to cashh $6	6.00
Oliver Nickerson	July 19th 1851 to three bushels wheat	$ 3.0

January 12th 1852   then balance accounts with Andrew
    McMannes remains due to said McMannes $ 85.25
                                                         $85.00

April 22 1852	Andrew McMannes Db to cash $6	6.00

		91.0

(new page)

June 14th 1806   Received of Jonathon Sauol cash paid the
same time for Susan Conklin   2-2-2

November 5th 1849 Susanan Wig began to work for A.I.C.
    Oliver Nickerson Db to AIC $00.00
    Db to cash for a pair of boots $.2.00
    Db to ½ bushel of corn $.o.30 cents

Susanan Db to three days lost Christmas to home   3

June 29th 1850	Oliver Nickerson Cr by 5 ½ days hoing	
	corn	5 ½
	Second week by 1 days work	1
	3rd week by 5 ½ days work in hay	5 ½
	4th week Cr by 4 days work	4
	5th week Cr by 4 days work	4
	6th week Cr by 3 ½ days work	3 ½
July - 16th 1852 Oliver Nickerson Cr by 5 days		---------
		23 ½
		5
		--------
		28 ½

November 18th 1850 Oliver Nickerson Db to cash $6.00

March 4th 1851 Maryann Beskins begun to work for A.I.C.

March 24th 1851   Maryann Db to cash six dollars $6.0

May 23rd 1851	Maryann Db to cash two dollars	$2.0
July 15th 1851	Maryann Db to cash seven dollars	$7.0
August 14th 1851	Maryann Db to cash Three dollars	$3.0
September 23rd 1851	Maryann Beskins Db to cash	$8.0
October 6th 1851	Maryann Db to cash $2	$2.0
October 29th 1851	Maryann Beskins Db to cash $9	$9.0
January 29th 1852	Maryann Brskins Db to cash $2	$2.0

Accounts with Mary Beskins March 1st 1852 $10
Received $10 cash in full

Maryan Beskins Db to cash $4 April 26th 1852 $4.0

May 8th 1852   Maryann Db to cash four dollars   4.0
Db to cash for 2 days work on the ?? (atosethomone) ??
                                                                                               ..33

June 12th 185   Maryan Db to cash $7   7.00

July 30th   Db to cash four dollars $4   4.00
Received payment in full $7.00

April 14th 1853   Andrews McMannes Db to Abraham I
Conklin
To cash $0 dollars

(new page)

William Conklin Db to Abraham I Conklin to cash

April 2 d 1808   Cash paid unto N Austin for schooling
                                                                    0-15-0

September 15   Cash paid to Vancunon for schooling
                                                               0-16-0

	Cash paid to N Basley for William schooling	0-12-2
C	Db Cash paid N Basley for William Schooling	0-17-8
	Db William Timlon for Schooling	0-7-0
	Db to Wright Lattin	0-8-0
	Db to Howlet for William Schooling	0-8-3
	Db to Howlet for Schooling	0-5-6
	Db cash paid to Bleaksley for schooling	0-6-0
	Cash paid to Cash for William	0-16-0

		5-11-7

January 10th 1853 Maryann Beskins begun to work for
    Abraham I Conklin

April 4th 1853	Maryann Db to six dollars	$6.0
	Db April 16th Db to cash $1	$1.0
	Db April 31 th Db to cash six dollars	$6.0

June 6th 1853   Maryann Db to 9 dollars $9.0

Received payment in full June 6th 1853

(new page)
(scratch pad with various calculations and random notations)

e.g. S note of 75				June 23 15
Frich notes				
1795 Patterson	125			July 5
Henry Fowlins note	50 $1802			
? ecmling 1802	50 1802			

	7

	3.50
	(calculations)

July | 5 75
| | 22.97
| | -------
| | 97.97
| | - 15
| | ------
| | 82.97
| | 5.31
| | --------
| | 88.28
| | - 1.50
| | -----------
| | 86.78
| | 3.50
| | ----------
| | 90.28
| | - 9
| | --------
| | 81.28
| | 5.68
| | ---------
| | 86.96
| | - 9
| | --------
| | 77.96
| | 10.70
| | ---------
| | 88.86
| | - 10.70
| | ---------
| | 78.86

　　　　　　5.52
　　　　　　84.88
　　　　　　- 19

　　　　　　65.38
　　　　　　31.99

　　　　　　$ 97.37
　　　Mors note of 15th

(new page)

Received Hyde Park November 4th 1846 of Abraham I Conklin fifty nine dollars and seventy cents in full for labor for seven months work

Isaac F Cliff $59.30

(new page)

Barge ticket receipt   W.Hunt & Co.
　　　　　　　　　　　The Barge Po'keepsie
　　　　　　　　　　　Lower landing   D.E.Hoffman
　　　　　　　　　　　　　Sold for A I Conklin
I d Trip July 8 1845

Received Poughkeepsie July 4th 1796 of John J Conklin one pound, one shilling 4 in full for board and shingles bought of Hendrick & Everet Pells

Pound 1 – S 1- 4 p   signed Hendrick Pells

(new page)

August 29th 1800　　　Hendrick Acker to making one suit of
　　close　　　　　　　　　　　　　　　　　　　1-4-0
　　Db to three scains silk & thread sticks twist　　0-3-0

January 7th 1801　　　Hendrick Acker to making one suit of
　　close Db 1.6.0 to thread and buttons 1 / 4　　1-7-4

　　　　　　　　　　　　　　　　　　　　　　　2-14-4

(new page)

April 3 d 1830　　　John Firce ?? Db to Abrm I Conklin

April 3 d 1830　　　to one stack of hay six dollars　　$ 6-0-0

June 5 th 1830　　　one hundred bales $5　　　　　　5-0-0

May 4 th 1831　　　to one bushel of seed corn &　　-62 ½ -0
　　Db to one bushel of seed buckwheat　　　　　　-50-0

June 4 th 1832　　　Db to one hundred bales $5　　5-0-0

September 3rd 1831　Daniel Lattin Cr by 5 days work　D 5

September 3rd 1831　Adolph lattin Cr by 3 ½ days work

　　Fs one load of wood price $3 per L　　　　3.0.0
　　Second　　Do　　　　　　　　　　　　　3.0.0
　　third　　　Do　　　　　　　　　　　　　3.25
　　fourth　　 Do　　　　　　　　　　　　　3.12 ½
　　fifth　　　 Do　　　　　　　　　　　　　3.00
　　sixth　　　Do　　　　　　　　　　　　　3.00
　　seventh　　Do　　　　　　　　　　　　　3.12 ½
　　eighth　　 Do　　　　　　　　　　　　　3.50
　　ninth　　　Do　　　　　　　　　　　　　3.00
　　tenth　　　Do　　　　　　　　　　　　　3.00

eleventh	Do	3.12 ½
twelth	Do	3.25
thirteenth	Do	3.00
fourtheenth	Do	3.00
fiftheenth	Do	3.25
sisteenth	Do	3.12 ½
seventheenth	Do	3.00
eighteenth	Do	3.00
nineteenth	Do	3.00
twenty	Do	3.00
twentyone	Do	3.12 ½
twenytwo	Do	3.00
twentythree	Do	3.12 ½
twentyfour	Do	3.00
twenryfive	Do	3.00
twentysix	Do	3.25
twentyseven	Do	3.00
twentyeight	Do	3.75
twentynine	Do	3.00
thirty	Do	3.00

		92.20
31 st	load wood	3.00
32 d	load wood	3.00
33 d	load wood	3.00
34 th	load wood	3.00
35 th	load wood	3.25
36 th	load wood	3.25
37 th	load wood	3.00
38 th	load wood	3.00
39 th	load wood	3.00
40 th	load wood	3.00
41 st	load wood	3.00

		33.50

April 20 th 1828   Nathanel Lattin Db to Abraham I
Conklin to Sundays

to 10 lb of flax at 11 p per lb		0-9-4
to one bushel of seed corn 5 (shilling)		0-5-0
to six bushels of wheat at 1 4 (shilling)		4-4-0
Db to two axle tires		0-8-0
42 d	load of wood	3.00
43 d	load of wood	3.00
44 th	load of wood	3.00
45 th	load of wood	3.6
46 th	load of wood	3.12 ½
47 th	load of wood	3.00
48 th	load of wood	3.00
49 th	load of wood	3.00
50 th	load of wood	3.00
51 st	load of wood	3.12 ½
52 d	load of wood	3.00
53 d	load of wood	2.75
54 th	load of wood	3.00
55 th	load of wood	3.00
56 th	load of wood	3.00
57 th	load of wood	3.00
58 th	load of wood	3.00
59 th	load of wood`	3.00
60 th	load of wood	3.00

		57.6

(new page)

March th 14 1800   then receive a note of John J conklin to collect against John Gay principle and interest is six dollars if not collected the note is to be returned

received by me Abraham I Conklin

(seven lines of entry faded and not readable)

1. e.g. ???????
2. January 14 1791 by cash ??
3. January ?? 1791 by cash ??
4. December th 2 1791 to making a coat & vest
5. ????? June th 7 1788 to making ???
6. August th 10 1789 to making one ?????

(end of faded section date is questionable ??)

April 20 th 1828	Nathaniel Cr by 430 feet of plank at three dollars per foot	0-12.90
	Db to one peck flax seed at	37 ½
	to one order by Odell 28 planks for by tub	3.50

(new page)

October th 9 1798	William Loader Db by cash	2-1-1
December th 1 1798	William Loder Db by cash	0-8-0
March th 12 1799	Db by cash	1-4-0
January th 12 1800	Db by cash for buttons and cloath	0-3-3

March th 19 1801	then balance accounts between John J Conklin and William Lowder remains due to said Conklin eight Shillings	0-8-0
	Jacob vanderburgh Db November th 27 1800 by one quarter beef W at 91 at 4/p	1-10-4
	John Conklin Db to two bushels & half corn	

John Conklin Db to eleven bushels & peck Rye lent

 Cr to one half bushel rye   p ½

January th 6 1801   Cr by two bushels rye   2

February the 27 1801   Cr by eight bushels and 2 pecks rye

March th 20 1801   then balance accounts between John J Conklin and John Conklin remains due to John Conklin ten dollars   4-0-0

May 1 st 1809   received of Abraham Patterson (pound) 29. 17 (shilling) on a note of John J Conklin   29-17-0 Received by me Abraham I Conklin

---

(new page)

September th 13 1798 William Lowder Cr to two and half days work   2-1/2

September th 22   Cr to four days work   4

September th 29   Cr to six days work   6

October th 6   Cr to 4 ½   4 ½

October th 9   Cr to four days   4

---

                21 days
at six shillings per day makes (pound) 6-6-0

November th 5 1799   Cr to one days and half day of John Thorn

February th 8 1800   Cr to making one ?????

December th 29 1798	Abraham Kip Db to one pair shose	0-12-0
January th 5 1799	Db by cash 26.17	0-0-0
January th 12 1799	by cash	0-1-0
January th 15 1799	by cash	0-2-0
January th 19 1799	by one lb butter	0-1-8
January th 23 1799	by cash	0-0-6
January th 26 1799	Db by an order on manny & husnan ??	
		1-4-0
February th 16 1799	Db by Cash	0-1-0
February th 18 1799	Db by cash 10/ and 2/p in needles	0-12-6
Febry th 22 1799	Db by cash	0-1-0
March th 1 1799	Db by cash	0-2-0
March th 13 1799	to one pair shoos bought of Saguy	0-14-0
	Db to needles two dosen	0-1-6

		3-13-2
February th 7 1799	Cr to one days work	1
February th 16 1799	Cr to four and half days work	4 ½
February th 22 1799	Cr to three days and half	3 ½

May th 20 1799 then William Onoss began to work for John Conklin

---

November th 27 1800 Susannah Patterson CR to one heffer
                      6-0-0

May th 4 1801   to 2 bushels plaster   0-12-0

September th 16 1802 to two & ?? sixteen lbs of beef at 4 d
                      3-12-0

November 20th 1805 to one hog Wt 160 at 5.0 (shilling) per lb
                      4-0-0

December 9th 1806 to one hog Wt 255 at (pound) 3 per hundred
                      7-18-0

                      21-16-0
                      3

                      27

(new page)

An Account of Building

August th 29 1797 Daniel Forman Cr to one days work 0-5-0

September 18 th 1797 to 6 d nails 14 lbs at 1 / 2 ?? 0-16-11
  at the same time 10 lbs ?? at 1 / 4 per pound 0-13-4

September 29 th Isaac Forman Cr to one days work 0-5-0

October th 2   John Wood Cr to him and hors ¾ days
    work at 4 / ?   0-3-0

October th 5   Joseph Mead Cr him and boy to 3 days
    each (blanked out)   ?-?-?

October th 5   William Lattin Cr to ¾ of a days work
                                                     0-3-0

October th 6   Jeans Willbur Cr to ¾ of a days work
                                                     0-3-0
        pitch pine plank and shingles   12-12-6

October th 7   Abrahan Wood Cr to two days work at 8
    (shillings)   0-16-0

October th 10   Derrick Amberman Cr to two days work
                                                     0-8-0

October th 14   Joseph Mead & boy Cr to 6 days work
    (blanked out)   ?-?-?

October th 14   Jeans Cronk Cr to four days work   1-12-0

October th 13   Garret Benneway Cr to two days work
                                                    0-12-0

October th 12   Jeans Benway Cr to one days work   0-4-0

October th 16   Joseph Mead Cr him & boy each one day
    (blanked out)   ?-12-?

October th 16   Derrick Amberman Cr to one days work
                                                     0-4-0

October th 21	Eleser Chace Cr to one days work & batter ??	
		0-4-6
October th 27	Simon Fvaer Cr to two days masoning	
		0-16-0
October th 27	Abraham Wood Cr to one & half days masoning	
		0-12-0
October th 27	John Raymons Cr to one days masoning	
		0-12-0
October th 27	Garret Beneway Cr to one days work	
		0-6-0
October th 30	Jesse Smith Cr to one days work	0-11-6
October th 30	Garret Beneway Cr to one days work	
		0-6-0
November th 4	Joseph Mead & boy Cr to four days work each (crossed out)	
		2-12-0
November th 7	John Raynous Cr to half days work (no entry)	
November th 11	Joseph Mead & boy to six days each this is muds hoh a work?? (crossed out)	
November th 13	Meads boy Cr to one days wor (crossed out)	
		0-11-0
November th 14	Abraham Wood CR to day & half work	
		0-12-0
	plank of Richard Davis	1-0-6
	plank bought of Ring	1-2-7
	Bought of Cook 7 lbs nails at 1 / 4	0-12-0

(new page)

plank bought of Richard Davis	1-0-6
quarter boards bought of Ring	1-16-6

November th 27   Jeans Latchel Cr to ?/ing eleven hundred
&fifty lath at 6 shillings

per & ? thousand	iron 19 / 6	0-19-6
nails 8 lbs at 1 / 3		0-10-0

December th 9   Walter Grysel Cr to five days work 1-15-0

December th 16   Joseph Mead Db by cash (crossed out)
                                                                                          10-0-0
    on account of bricks   5-10-0

March th 5 1798   then paid John J Storm   3-4-0
    glass nails paint & boards   3-7-9

April th 21 1798   John Lawless Cr him & son 9 mdays each
                                                                                     6-6-0
    nails which William Lattin got & thum latches 0-10-2

April th 28 1798   Jim Fraer Cr him & mint him four days
April th 28 1798   and mint five days in whole   4-0-0
    cash paid to Fraer two pounds 2 shillings   2-2-0

April th 28 1798   Derrick Ambleman Cr to five days of
    work   1-5-0

April th 27 1798   lime bought of Casy Wt twice 26 bushels
    1 / 0   1-6-0

May th 22 1798   Daniel Forman Cr to half days work 0-3-0

May th 23 1798	William Loder Cr to one days work (no entry)	
July th 7 1798	to plank nails and iron	3-2-1
July th12 1798	to glass & hinges	1-2-0

    six lbs large nails at 1 / 2 per pound makes 7 (shillings)

	0-7-0
24 boards at 1 /2 makes	1-8-0
boards thum latches hinges & nails	0-16-6
William Loders work	6-6-0
Hendrick Leroys work	0-18-0
tutels ? For painting	0-14-0
on account of farnk ??	1-9-8
Joseph Mead & boys account	13-4-0
Db to Mead for sash	1-12-0

(new page)

Clinton April 9 1794

    Be it remembered by John Conklin & David Conklin & Isaac Conklin That John Conklin the decesse of Poughkeepsie was lawfully indebted to his son John Conklin in the sum of Pounds 5 at his decease which he has not yet received.

March th 2 1796 Forman	John Conklin Db by cash paid to Daniel	0-7-0
April th 7 1796	cash paid to Nathan Wigg	1-8-3
April th 13 1796	cash paid to Jeans Latchel	1-14-0
July th 4 1796	cash paid to Hendrick Pells for boards	1-1-4

August th 8 1796	paid to Derrick Ambleman for moing	0-11-0
August th 12 1796	to eighteen bushels brand at 2 /	1-16-0
August th 12	cash paid to Derrick Amberman to Thurston	0-16-0
August th 12 1796	paid to Thurston for Nankeen	1-5-5
	Cash paid to Sparrow for cash 7 / 6	0-7-6
August th 29 1796	Db by cash 25 dollars is	10-0-0
	cash paid to William Ely for plaster	0-8-0
	cash paid to Simon J Pells for cash	0-16-0
	cash paid to Abraham A Wood for hoing corn	0-3-6
	cash paid to peter ? Vanwagner	2-4-9
	one & quarter yds retinet ? At 4 /	0-5-0
	cash paid to Mindert Van Hleck ?? & son	0-16-8
	cash paid to Nat Wood	0-17-6
	cash paid for steel for their sled	1-2-8
	cash paid to carpenter for nails	0-11-8
	cash paid to Nathanel Wood for work at the barn (crossed out)	0-17-6

		26-12-3

May th 7 1801	Nathan Wigg Cr to weaving 36 1/3 yards of cloath at 1 /	1-16-9
	to weaving 13 yards I /	0-13-0
	to fourteen and half at 1 /	0-14-6
	to eleven and half at 1 /	0-11-6

(new page)

October th10 1795   then borrowed one hundred and ten
  dollars of John Conklin by me John J Conklin   44-0-0

February th 29 1796   John J Conklin Db to my father by cash
  thirty two pounds   32-0-0

October th 12 John Storm begun to work for one month
  Abraham Kip is to work at the rate of four dollars per
  month

January th 13 1798   Abraham Kip Cr to four days work   4

February th 20 1798   Cr to five days work   5

December th 22 1797   Cr to one day & half work   ½

February th 6 1799   Joseph Gran Cr by cash   0-8-0

Nathan Wigg Db March th 30 1801 to one and half bushel corn
  at 7 / 6   0-11-3

May th 7 1801 to 2 bushels corn at 6 / 6   0-13-0

November th 19 1801 to cash twenty shillings   1-0-0

November th 19 1801 Db to three bushels corn at 6 /   0-18-0
  Cr by flax 10 at 1/ 3 per pound   0-12-6

                                                         3-14-9

March th 22 1802   Balance accounts between John J Conklin and
  Nathan Wigg remains due to said Wigg one pound   1-0-0

March th 5 1798	John J Storm Db by cash	1-7-3

January th 6 1801   Derrick Amberman Db to one bushel
    corn (no entry)

October th 14	John Storm lost half day (no entry)	
October th 14	Db by cash eight shillings	0-8-0
October th 24	to half day lost (no entry)	
November th 11	John Storm time was out (no entry)	
	Db to two dosen buttens	0-2-0
	Db to 6 scains thread	0-0-6
November th 27	to one hat cover	0-4-0

		1-6-6
May th 13 1797	Joseph Thorn Cr to ten pounds flax at 1 / 6	
		-15-
October th 11	Derrick Ambleman Db by cash	0-2-0
October th 13	Db by cash	0-2-0

(new page)

November th 2 1793	John Wood Db to one and quarter wool at	
2 /		0-2-6
	to two bushels buckwheat at 2 / 6	0-5-0
November th 6 1793	to two bushels wheat at 8 / 6	0-17-0
February th 10 1794	Db to three bushels buckwheat at 2 / 6	
		0-7-6

April th 11 1794	Db to three pounds cash	3-0-0

April th 15 1794	Db to two hundred of hay at 3 /	0-6-0
	to two bushels of wheat at 8 /	0-16-0
	to two bushels rye at 4 / 6	0-9-0
	to ten pounds flax at / 10	0-8-4
	June th 7 1794 by cash	1-4-0

November th18 1795 this account settled off   7-15-4

December th 24 1795 then paid Nathaniel Wood on my fathers
        account by me John J Conklin   1-0-0

September th 24 179? Willaim Stoutenburgh Cr by cash   0-8-0

February th 19 1796   by cash eight shillings   0-8-0

January th 4 1796 Robert Welsh begun to work with John J
     Conklin

On account of rye August th 19 Tunis Tappan Db to one hundred
        weight rye flour   1-2-0

John Conklin Db to eighteen bushels brand at 8 /   1-16-0

Thomas Warren Db to one bushel brand at 4 /   0-4-0

Derrick Ambleman to half hundred of flour   0-11-0

Eseckel Binkney to one bushel brand at 2 /   0-2-0

Charles Justin to eight bushels brand at 2 /   0-16-0

John Hunt Db to four bushels brand at 2 /		0-8-0
Abijah Batterson Db to four and half bushels at 2 /		0-9-0
One ?? pasel ry flour sold for 2-10-6		2-10-6

December th 27 1798 then Abraham Kip begun to work for John J Conklin and is to work at the rate of forty shillings per month

December th 22 1798	Cr to five and half days work	5 ½
Decber th 29 1798	Cr to 6 days work	6
January th 5 1799	Cr to five days work	5
January th 12 1799	Cr to five & half days work	5 ½
January th 25 1799	Cr to five days work	5
February th 2 1799	Cr to four days work	4
February th 5 1799	Cr to ½ days work	1 ½

(new page)

Clinton April th 29 1794
   then balance accounts between John J Conklin & John D Conklin remains due to John J Conklin   1-2-8

Credit by going on interest Cr John J Storm (pound)   0-12-0

Robard Welch Dr to John J Conklin by cash   0-3-0

February th 6 1796	by cash	0-3-0

February th 13 1796 then balance accounts between John J Conklin & Roberd Welch remains due to Welch   0-12-0

March th 9 1796	Henry Lake credit by his father	0-5-0
March th 21 1796	Cr by cash of himself	0-19-0
April th 11 1797	by cash	0-16-0

October th 10 1796 then Abraham Kip begun to work for seven months at one pound two shillings per month

October th 15 1796   Abraham Kip Db to half day lost to go to the hors race (no entry)

October th 25 1796	Db to one vest	0-12-0
October th 25 1796	Db by cash	0-4-0
October th 25 1796	to one day lost (no entry)	

Novemeber th 30 1796	to one hankerchief	0-8-0
	to one pair stockings	0-9-0
	to one knife	0-2-0
	to one pocket hankerchief	0-3-3
	to cash	0-1-0
	to cash	0-?-6
January th 14 1796	to one notch block	0-3-0
	to one dosen needles	0-1-0

January th 14 1797	to half bushel corn at 8 /	0-4-0
January th 21 1797	to one bushel rye at 8 /	0-8-0
January th 26 1797	by cash	0-0-6
February th 4 1797	by cash	0-1-0
February th 16 1797	to soling one seathes ??	0-3-0
March th 21 1797	Db by cash	0-4-0

Db by cash six shillings in two payments three shillings at a time   0-6-0

(new page)

February th 13 1792 then balance accounts between John J Conklin and Gilbert Conklin remains due to John J Conklin the sum of one pound five shillings & eight pence going on interest (pound) 1=5=8

interest for the same 0-1-9

1-7-5

February th 18	Gilbert Conklin credit by cash	0-9-0

May th 12 1794   Isaac Conklin credit to two yards & half & half quarter linning at 3 / 6   0-9-2

August th 21 1795   Nathan Wigg Db to 1 bushel & peck rye

0-11-3

September th 23 1795   to one bushel rye at 8 shillings   0-8-0

October th 16 1795   to one and half bushels rye at 8 /   0-12-0

December th 16 1795 to two bushels buckwheat at 4 /   0-8-0

December th 23 1795 to one shoat weighing 51 and half at 3 / 2
                                                                                           0-15-0

    Abraham Kip lost time

January th 16 1797   to one day lost

January th 21 1797   to one day lost

February th 2 1797   to four days lost

February th 7 1797   to one & half days lost

February th 14 1797   to one & half days lost
    Credit to half days work

February th 14 1797   then Abraham Kip went away

January th 10 1798   then Abraham Kip begun to work with John J Conklin by the month for (pound) 1=12 per month

---

March th 23 1798   Rebard Welch Cr to five days work

March th 23 98   Db by cash twelve shillings

---

    the widow Latchel Db to 21 ? pound pork at / 9   0-8-0

   Db to four pound beef at / 4   0-1-4

(new page)

October th 11 1791   John Conklin Db to John J Conklin three bushels salt at 3 / 9   0-11-3

September 1 1792   John D Conklin Credit by three bushels wheat of his brother Abram sold for six & ten pence makes   1-0-6
     freight & half measuring to come out   0-0-10

                                                                   ..-19-8

August th 17 1793   then balance accounts between John Conklin and John Ward remains due to John Ward five pounds five shillings and three pence   5-5-3

       Abraham Kip lost Time

October th 15 96   to half day lost

October th 25 1796   to one day lost

November th 14 1796   to half day lost

December th 2 1796   to two days lost

December th 17 1796   to eight days lost

December th 22 1796   to three days lost

December th 18 96   to five days lost

December th 28 1796   to five days lost

January th 5 1797   to four days lost

January th 14 1797   to one and half day lost

November th 2 1795   Daniel Forman Db to John J Conklin
    sixteen & five pence   0-16-5

September th 22   Ive began to sow the hill and 23 went to
    till the 26

John J Conklin is to pay Philip Irish two shillings and eight pence
    for Francis Lery ?   0-2-8

---

    paid 8 / 4 to John Ward for my father November th 18
    1795 by me John J Conklin paid to Elijah Wright 3-8-0
    for my father John Conklin   3-8-0

    Joseph Thorn Db on Samuel Lewis account to John J
    Conklin   2-4-9

    September 1795 the 23 we begun to sow

(new page)

December th 5 1791   then balance account stood on John J
    Conklin and Jacob Bartley remains due to John J Conklin 4 /
                                                      0-4-0

August th 3 1792   John Gay Db by cash thirty shillings
                                                          1-10-0

March th 19 1793   John Bartick Db to seven gallons sider at
     one shilling pr gallon   0-7-0

August th 27 1792   George Happey credit by cash fifteen
     shillings and and eight pence   0-15-8

February th 21 1793   balance due from John Odell   0-12-0

July th 9 1794 Francis begun to work here for one month at the
     rate of three pounds   3-0-0
     John Conklin

August ? 1795 then Francis Leroy begun to work here for two
     months he is to have------------------------------------
                                                                7-5
     he begun the middle of the afternoon

Joseph Wood	Db 2 lbs flax at 10 d per lb	0-18-4
April th 12 1797	Ely Angevine Cr by cash	0-17-0
John Vanderburgh work November th 11 1798		1-9-0
2 coats & breeches and trowsers ??siach		

June th 9 1794   Joshua Moss credit by cash   1-0-0

August th 23 1794   credit by cash   0-8-9
     August th 25 1794 by cash   0-10-0
     this John J Conklin ???

August th 27 1792 then (John) balance accounts between John J Conklin and Johnny Odell remains due to John J Conklin fifteen and eight pence   0-15-8

February th 24 1793   John Odell Db to making coat and breeches   0-16-0

1-11-7

February the 21 1793 credit by cash (pound) 0-12-0   0-12-0
John Odell by cash 0-7-0   0-12-7
balance due from John Odell (pound)   0-9-0

(new page)

Cure for bone spaven
to 1 gill of oil of spike ?
To 1 gill of spirits of turpentine
to 1 tea spoon full ? of salt petre

Recigsit ?? for the ring bone
burn the callace in three places
pitch pine turpentine bees wax
rosen mutton tallow to 1 gill of
oil of spike to 1 gill of the spirits of turpentine

---

cure for the stiffle

take the white of six eggs to ½ lb of cynece ?
Mix them together & bathe it in with
hot brich till all used up

END

Index of Names Appearing in the Account Book
September 1791 Through July 1823

The entering are alphabetical by activity. The activities are:
1) Tailor / clothing sales
2) Farm customers
3) Financial / Notes, debts
4) Farm workers
5) Building project
6) Vendors
7) School masters

The enteries following the name refers to the page on which the name appears, multiple pages indicate multiple activities.

Tailoring Business

Acker, Hendrick 43, 43, 47, 48, 71
Ackerman, Jeams 28
Amberman, Derick 37
Angvine, Jonathon 16, 19, 21
    Ely 31, 34
Apells, Hendrick 32, 33
Ausber, Polerd 44
Badgley, Joshua 45, 46
Baker, Samuel 41, 51
Balding, William 16
    Isaac 24, 27
Barlow, Abijah 36, 36
    Bige 46
Barns – Barnes
    Joshua 48, 52
    William 41, 49
    David 49
Bartley, Jacob 15
Beneway, Jacobus 34
    Esekel 50
Bennet, Efram 29
Bostick, John 20
Cain, John 35, 36
Carmon, John 17
Casy, Thomas 32, 33, 36, 36, 39, 39

Chan, William 47
Church, John 16, 18
Churchel, John 17
Conklin, Abraham D 16, 25, 28
    Abraham I 44
    David 15, 16, 17, 19, 19, 20, 20, 20, 21, 21, 22, 23, 23, 24, 26, 26
    Isaac 16, 17, 21, 23, 27, 38, 44, 46, 47, 47, 88
    John 14, 41, 42
    John D 17
    Richard 18
    Tunis 32, 40
Cook, William 17
Coon, Jesse 31
Cronk, Jeams 31, 33, 35
Culver, John 27, 27, 37
    Jeams 30
    Jeans 27
Delren, Daniel 48
Disbrow, Henry 41
Donlon – Dorlon, Benjamin 21, 26
Dusberry, Henry 33
Echer – Eckert, Hendrick 19, 19
Flagler, Paul 24
Flow, John 22
Foreman – Forman, Isaac 38
    Daniel 40
Golder, John 20, 21, 22, 24, 27, 46
Gooden, John J 44
Gorder, John 25
Green, Joseph 26, 35, 38, 42
Hall, John 16
Hallick, Elijah 51
Happy, George 17

Hoocon, Bot 16
Hunt, John 19, 46, 48, 48
Husted, Joseph 18
Hutchins, Isaac 38
    Jacob 25, 28, 30
Irish, Phillip 30, 40, 44, 48
Justice, Charles 25
Kilsey, Jony 42, 42
King, David 28, 47
Lake, Henry 27, 29, 45
    Jeams 34
    John 45
Latchel – Latcher – Lathel
    James 52
    Jeams 29, 29, 32, 32, 34, 37, 37, 39, 39, 40, 46, 46, 50, 50, 52
    William 41, 42, 43, 50
Latten – Lattin – Latting – Latton
    Benjamin 14, 19, 29
    Dolph 43, 43
    Lief 22
    Nathaniel 38, 46
    Silas 13
    William 25, 36, 39
Lattony, Nathaniel 41
Lawlis – Lawless, John 33, 39
Lewis, Charles 30
    Samuel 18, 19, 22, 23, 35
Loder – Lowder – Lauder
    William 42, 42, 46, 47, 49, 50, 51

Lowel, Jonathan 27
Manning, Caleb 32
    Charles 16, 21, 21, 26, 28,
        30, 49, 23
    Jacob 28, 29, 33, 35
    John 26
Mead, Joseph 38, 4
Meeks, Ellick 29
Milkins, Robert 18
Mors – Moss – Moro
    Elijah 24
    Joshua 23, 24, 25, 33
    Nathaniel 29, 24
Mott, Joseph 18, 20, 21
Nash, Philip 23
Nelson, David 30
Newkerk, John 32
Night, Jeams 37, 40
Odell, John 16, 20, 93
Owen, Jonathan 31, 33, 34
Palmer, William 33
Patterson – Petteron
    Abram 50
    Abraham 48, 51
    John 26, 42, 43
Pells, Hendrick 35, 36
    Simon 35
Pellse, Prime 18
Petel, Deter 26
Philips, George 31
Platt, Joseph 35
Porlin, Benjamin 27
Reccord, John 39
Reelding, Samuel 45
Rider, Theodorus 25, 29
Right, Elijah 27, 28, 29, 30, 30

Ring, David 38
Schuryver – Schriver,
    Albartis 16
    Peter 13, 17, 35, 36
    William 20
    ??? 15
Sagues – Segues – Sigue
    John 39, 43, 45
    Johny 39
    Samuel 38
Shear, Lewis 18, 19
Silvernale – Silvernail –
    Silvernails
    John 27
    Winant 24
    Winat 27
    Winot 17
Smith, Samuel 26, 28
Sowl, Jonathon 22, 23, 49,
50, 50, 51
Spenser, Matthew 31
Stoutenbough, James W 18
    William 17, 24, 30
Storm – Storms
    Francis 17, 22, 34
    James S 42
    James 13, 19
    Jeams P 42
    Jeams 13, 14, 32,
        33, 34, 35, 43, 52
    John J 36, 37, 38
    John 18
    Joseph 49
    Peter 13, 15, 21, 22
        25, 25, 27, 28, 31
Taylor, Reberd 44

Tarpanny – Tarpanning
    John 20
    Simon 22
Thurston, John M 30
    Joseph 31
    Samuel 49
Thorn, John 50, 51, 52
    Joseph 37, 40, 40, 46, 47, 48, 50, 51
    Stephen 22
Thuylon, John M 48
Tod, William 22
Tompkins – Tomkins, Mikel 15
    Mike 20
Travis, Isaac 15, 31, 31, 34, 38, 43, 47, 50, 51
    John Jur 13
    John J 28
    John 47
Tuttles, James 18
Valentine, James 23
Vall, James 15
Vananden – Venandon
    Aron 45
    Nicholas 37
Vanearey, Jacob 15
Vandewater, Benjamin 47
Vanderburgh, John 92
Van Wagner, Peter 20, 34
Waff, Laweance 23
Ward, John 22
Weeks, Jesse 40, 43
    Joseph 41

Wig – Wigg
    John Jur 15
    Nathan 15, 19, 23, 30, 37
Wilbur, James 23, 23
    Jeams 24, 32
    Jeanis 29
    Jeans 21
    Silvenus 33
Wilsy, ?? 34
Wiles, Jeams 35
Williams, Richbel 37, 40
    William 39
Witman, Thomas 37
Wood, Abram Jr 26
    Abraham A 42, 45, 45, 49, 51
    Abraham 40
    Isaac 25, 36
    John 24, 31, 41, 44, 44, 48
    Nathaniel 28, 32, 34, 36
Wright, Elijah 51

Farm Customers

Amberman, Derrick 84, 85
Angevine, Ely 57
Bartick, John 92
Batterson, Abijah 86
Binkney, Essekel 85
Conklin, John D 90
    John 14, 74, 75, 85, 90
Firce, John 71
Gran, Joseph 83
Hunt, John 86
Justin, Charles 85
Latchel, Widow 89
Lowder – Louder – Loder
    William 74

Lattin, Nathaniel 73
    Susan 57
Odell, Nathan 74
Patterson, Susannah 77
Schuryer, Peter 14
Tappan, Tunis 85
Thorn, John 75
    Joseph 84
Vandeeburgh, Jacob 74
Van dewater, W 54
Wright, 58, 60, 61, 62
Warren, Thomas 85
Wigg, Nathan 82, 83, 88
Wood, John 84

Finance / Notes / Debts

Amberman, Derrick 82, 84
Angevine, Ely 92
Bartley, Jacob 91
Conklin, David 81
    Gilbert 88
    Isaac 81, 88
    John D 86
    John J 14, 73, 74, 75, 83,
    85, 86, 87, 88, 91, 93
    John 75, 81, 83, 90, 91
Cliff, Isaac F 70
Cullin, Samuel 57
Dubois, Anthony 54
Forman, Daniel 91
Fowlins, Henry 68
Frich, 68
Gay, John 73, 91

Gran, Joseph, 83
Happey, George 92
Irish, Philip 91
Latchel, 14
Latten – Latting
    Benjamin 14
    Sias 13
    Susan 57
Lattin, Daniel 57
Lake, Henry 87
Lewis, Samuel 91
Lowder, William 74
Moss, Joshua 92
Odell, John 92, 93
    Nathan 53, 54, 55
Patterson, Abraham 75
Pells, Hendrich 70

Platt, Daniel 54
, ?? 68
Sauol, Jonathon 66
Storm, Francis 13
    James 13
    Jeams 13
    John J 84, 86
    Peter 13
Stautenburgh, William 85

Thorn, Joseph 91
Travis, Isaac 15
    John Jr 13
VandeWater, W 54
Ward, John 90, 91
Welch, Robard 86, 87
Wigg, Nathan 81
Wood, Nathaniel 85
Wright, Elijah 91

Workers

Beskins, Maryann 61, 66, 67, 68
Clark, Eliza 61
Cliff, Isaac F 70
Cooper, Elazon 58
DuBois, Anthony 53, 54
    Lewis 63, 64
England, Eliza 60, 61, 62
Freigtenburgh, Jonah 57
Kip, Abraham 76, 83, 86, 87, 89, 90
Lattin, Adolph 71
    Daniel 71
Leroy, Francis 92
Lowder – Loder, William 75, 81
McManney - McWilliams
    Andrew 63, 64, 65, 66, 67

Murphy, Mary 65
Nickerson, Oliver 58, 59, 60, 65, 66
Onoss, William 77
Storm, John 83, 84
Thorn, John 75
Welsh, Robert 85, 89
Wig, Susan 65
    Susannan 66
Wilber, Samuel 59
Wood, Abraham 78, 79, 82
    John 60, 78, 84
    Joseph 60
    William 58

Building Project

Amberman, Derrick 78, 80, 82
Benneway, Garret 78, 79
Jeans 78
Casy, 80

Chace, Eleser 79
Cook 79
Cronk, Jeans 78
Davis, Richard 79, 80

Ely, William 82
Forman, Daniel 77, 80, 81
    Isaac 77
Fraer, Jim 80
    Simon 79
Lawless, John 80
Leroys, Hendrick 81
Loder, William 81
Mead, Joseph 78, 79, 80, 81
    Nathaniel 74
Pells, Everet 70
    Hendrick 70, 81
    Simon J 82
Raymons, John 79
Raynous, John 79
Ring, 79, 80

Grysel, Walter 80
Latchel, Jeans 80, 81
Lattin, William 78, 80
Smith, Jesse 79
Sparrow, 82
Storm, John J 80
Tutels, 81
Van Hleck, Mindert 82
Van Wagner, Peter 82
Wilbur, Jeans 78
Wood, Abraham 78, 79
    John 78
    Nathaniel 82
    Nat 82

Vendors

W.Hunt Co 70
Fuld, Benjamin 56
Kip, Abraham 76
Odell, 74
Pells, Everet 70
    Henrdick 70

Saguy, 76
Shoemaker 64
Thurston 82
Wigg, Nathan 82

School Masters

Conklin, Susan 66
    William 67
Austin, N 68
Basley, N 68
Bleaksley, ? 68

Howlet, ? 68
Lattin, Wright 68
Shear, Lewis 18
Timlon, William 68
Vancunon, ? 68

About the Author

Jack Conklin grew up on the family farm where this account book was discovered. The property was in the Conklin family for 7 generations and 220 years. Located the easternmost part of the town of Hyde Park, the original farm boundaries formed the lines of the Dutchess County Towns of Pleasant Valley, Poughkeepsie and Hyde Park.

Jack is a graduate of West Point, Class of 1956, and a retired businessman who was President of several local businesses. He has authored articles for the Historical Societies of Dutchess County and Rhinebeck, as well as writing a history column for a local newspaper.

This publication makes available, to interested genealogists, the hundreds of names recorded in the 1791 Conklin Farm account book.

John R. Conklin
Rhinecliff, NY

www.ingramcontent.com/pod-product-compliance
Lightning Source LLC
Chambersburg PA
CBHW060033180426
43196CB00045B/2653